MAKERS
of the
MUSLIM
WORLD

'Abd al-Mu'min

TITLES IN THE MAKERS OF THE MUSLIM WORLD SERIES

Series Editors: Professor Khaled El-Rouayheb, Harvard University, and Professor Sabine Schmidtke, Institute for Advanced Study, Princeton

'Abd al-Ghani al-Nabulusi, Samer Akkach
'Abd al-Malik, Chase F. Robinson
Abd al-Rahman al-Kawakibi, Itzchak Weismann
'Abd al-Rahman III, Maribel Fierro
'Abd al-Rahman b. 'Amr al-Awza'i, Steven C. Judd
Abu Nuwas, Philip F. Kennedy
Ahmad al-Mansur, Mercedes García-Arenal
Ahmad ibn Hanbal, Christopher Melchert
Ahmad ibn Tulun, Matthew S. Gordon
Ahmad Riza Khan Barelwi, Usha Sanyal
Aisha al-Ba'uniyya, Th. Emil Homerin
Akbar, André Wink
Al Ma'mun, Michael Cooperson
Al-Mutanabbi, Margaret Larkin
Amir Khusraw, Sunil Sharma
Ashraf 'Ali Thanawi, Muhammad Qasim Zaman
Beshir Agha, Jane Hathaway
Chinggis Khan, Michal Biran
Elijah Muhammad, Herbert Berg
Fazlallah Astarabadi and the Hurufis, Shahzad Bashir
Ghazali, Eric Ormsby
Hasan al-Banna, Gudrun Krämer
Husain Ahmad Madani, Barbara D. Metcalf
Ibn 'Abd al-Wahhab, Michael Crawford
Ibn 'Arabi, William C. Chittick
Ibn 'Asakir of Damascus, Suleiman A. Mourad
Ibn Hamdis the Sicilian, William Granara
Ibn Taymiyya, Jon Hoover
Ibn Tufayl, Taneli Kukkonen
Ikhwan al-Safa', Godefroid de Callataÿ
Imam Shafi'i, Kecia Ali
Karim Khan Zand, John R. Perry
Mehmed Ali, Khaled Fahmy
Mu'awiya ibn Abi Sufyan, R. Stephen Humphreys
Muhammad Abduh, Mark Sedgwick
Mulla Sadra, Sayeh Meisami
Nasser, Joel Gordon
Nazira Zeineddine, Miriam Cooke
Sa'di, Homa Katouzian
Shah 'Abbas, Sholeh A. Quinn
Shaykh Mufid, Tamima Bayhom-Daou
Usama ibn Munqidh, Paul M. Cobb
'Uthman ibn 'Affan, Heather N. Keaney

For current information and details of other books in the series, please visit oneworld-publications.com/makers-of-the-muslim-world

MAKERS
of the
MUSLIM
WORLD

‘Abd al-Mu’min

Mahdism and Caliphate in the Islamic West

MARIBEL FIERRO

ONEWORLD
ACADEMIC

Oneworld Academic

An imprint of Oneworld Publications

Published by Oneworld Academic in 2021

A CIP record for this title is available from the British Library

ISBN 978-1-85168-428-1
eISBN 978-0-86154-192-8

'Arabic genealogy of Ibn Tumart and 'Abd al-Mu'min' adapted from Maribel Fierro, 'Las genealogías de 'Abd al-Mu'min, primer califa almohade', *Al-Qanṭara* 24 (2003), 77–108. English translation in M. Fierro, *The Almohad Revolution. Politics and Religion in the Islamic West During the Twelfth–Thirteenth Centuries*, Ashgate, 2012, v.

Maps 2 and 3 prepared by the Unidad SIGyHD (CCHS-CSIC).

Typeset by Geethik Technologies
Printed and bound in Great Britain by Clays Ltd, Elcograf S.p.A.

Oneworld Publications
10 Bloomsbury Street
London WC1B 3SR
England

To my son Andrés

CONTENTS

FOREWORD

This is a book about a man from the Berber Zanata tribe who in the first half of the twelfth century played a special role in events that altered the history of the Maghrib, al-Andalus (Muslim Iberia) and the Western Mediterranean. His name was 'Abd al-Mu'min and, from humble beginnings, he rose to become the leader of a new religious and political movement, that of the Almohads (*al-muwahhidun*) – the 'Unitarians', so-called because of their belief in the uncompromising Unity of God (*al-tawhid*). From 1130 to 1269, the Almohads ruled an empire that at its peak stretched from what is today southern Morocco to the southern part of the Iberian Peninsula and from the Atlantic to Tripoli (Libya).

'Abd al-Mu'min's own life had been changed by his encounter with the doctrinal founder of the Almohad movement, Ibn Tumart, a Masmuda Berber from the Sus, the southern region of what is now Morocco, whose followers came to consider him the Mahdi, a Messianic figure. These followers were mostly Masmuda tribesmen led by their shaykhs (elders, notables).

Before going on, it might be useful to explain some of the terms used above. The Maghrib is an Arabic term meaning 'the West', generally used to refer to the lands of North Africa west of Egypt: today's Libya, Tunisia (in Arabic, Ifriqiya), Algeria (al-Maghrib al-awsat, the central Maghrib) and Morocco (al-Maghrib al-aqsa, the far Maghrib). 'Abd al-Mu'min was born in a village near Nedroma in what is now western Algeria, while his teacher Ibn Tumart was born in Igiliz, in the Anti-Atlas Mountains.

Berber is our rendering of the Arabic term *barbar*, used in the Arabic sources to refer to the indigenous populations of North Africa who spoke local forms of the same language, referred to by modern linguists as Berber. One such form is Tachelhit, spoken in the Sus region. The term *barbar* was used in a derogatory sense, as in the Greek *barbaroi* and in the Latin *barbari*, to refer to peoples who spoke a language that sounded strange, and were thus considered to be uncivilized. In the Arabic sources, the Berbers are usually portrayed negatively, as rebels who resisted the Arab conquest and the process of Arabization (adoption of the Arabic language), and whose Islamization (conversion and acculturation to Islam) often followed trends such as Kharijism, Isma'ili Shi'ism and Almohadism that were considered deviant by 'mainstream' Sunni Muslims. The term Berber does not reflect the way those to which it referred viewed themselves. This in-group view is difficult to reconstruct today because of the scarcity of literary records in their spoken language, but they appear to have viewed themselves primarily as attached to specific tribal groupings, such as the Zanata, into which 'Abd al-Mu'min was born; the Masmuda, Ibn Tumart's tribe; and the Sanhaja, to which the rulers of the time, the Almoravids, belonged.

The Mahdi, an Arabic term that means 'the Rightly Guided One', is a Messianic figure with an eschatological dimension; he is supposed to appear at the end of days to restore justice and fight the Dajjal (Antichrist). This eschatological Mahdi is generally considered to be a descendant of the Prophet Muhammad. While belief in the Mahdi is found among Sunnis, it is especially developed among Shi'is, for whom genealogical charisma and eschatology are especially important. The term *mahdi*, more generally, refers to a man endowed with a superior type of knowledge that gives him access to the Truth in a way denied to ordinary human beings.

While *al-tawhid* (the belief in the Unity of God) is a central tenet of Islam, it can be formulated in different ways – in relation to God's attributes, for example. The Almohads or 'Unitarians' were known for their uncompromising conception of God's unity, in opposition to what they deemed to be the anthropomorphic deviation of their enemies, the Almoravids. Under 'Abd al-Mu'min's rule, scholars loyal to the dynasty were trained to teach and spread the Almohad *tawhid*. These scholars were called *talaba* (students; singular *talib*), and attached to the Mu'minid caliph and princes, the sayyids, who were the descendants of 'Abd al-Mu'min in charge of running the Almohad empire.

Throughout this book, Arabic terms are given in their most common Romanized form, without diacritics, with the exception of the *'ayn*, represented as ' and the *hamza* when it is not the initial position, represented as '. Berber terms and names are also rendered without exhaustive transliteration, according to their most common form.

Dates are given according to the Christian calendar. Sometimes they are rendered as, for example, 1106–7; in the Muslim lunar calendar (or hijra calendar, starting in 622, the year of Muhammad's migration from Mecca to Medina), if no specific date is given within a year, the latter may begin in one solar year and end in the following. Thus, the hijra year 500 corresponds to the years 1106–7 CE (starting on 2 September 1106 and ending on 21 August 1107).

The translation of the Qur'anic verses is that of Arthur John Arberry (as found at http://tanzil.net/) with some changes according to the context. The main sources are discussed in Chapters 2 and 7.

This book was inspired by the research conducted within the Advanced Research Grant *Knowledge, heresy and political culture in the Islamic West (Eighth–fifteenth centuries)*, European Research Council, Grant Agreement 229703 (2009–2014). It was written during Spain's Covid-19 lockdown from March to June 2020, as well as through summer 2020, after the lockdown was lifted. I am very grateful to the personnel of the Biblioteca Tomás Navarro Tomás and to Lourdes Martín-Forero Morente for their support. Many colleagues helped me in one way or another, among them Bilal Amroune, Carlos de Ayala, Xavier Ballestín, Umberto Bongianino, Pascal Buresi, Alejandro García Sanjuán, Mehdi Ghouirgate, Tawfiq Ibrahim, María Antonia Martínez Núñez, Aurélien Montel, Alejandro Peláez, Mounir Saifi, Jan Thiele, Houari Touati, and Jean-Pierre van Staëvel. Luis Molina's assistance has been invaluable. I wish also to thank the Association El Mouahidia, Nedroma (Algeria), for their kind help. Nicholas Callaway as always did more than a linguistic revision of the text: with his questions and suggestions he also improved it. Thanks also go to Jonathan Bentley-Smith and all those at Oneworld who have made this book possible. My deep gratitude to them all. I also owe special thanks to my son Andrés, with whom I spent the confinement and who, as always, was supportive and patient with my dedication to Almohad matters.

1

'ABD AL-MU'MIN, THE ZANATA BERBER WHO BUILT AN EMPIRE AND BECAME PRINCE OF THE BELIEVERS

Although largely ignored outside the field of the history of the Islamic West, 'Abd al-Mu'min should be counted among the great conquerors and builders of empires. As such – and also because of the violence employed against his foes – some of the Western scholars who have studied his biography have compared him to Charlemagne. The caliphate that 'Abd al-Mu'min established was not the first in the region, but it was more geographically vast than those that had preceded it, i.e. the caliphate of the Cordoban Umayyads and that of the Fatimids before their departure to Egypt. It did not last as long as that of the Umayyads (some 140 years as against 276), but its impact on the region is comparable.

'Abd al-Mu'min's accomplishments were many. After defeating the Almoravids and conquering their capital Marrakesh, he united the whole of North Africa west of Egypt, as well as parts of al-Andalus, for the first time. A member of a Zanata Berber tribe, he adopted the caliphal title of Prince of the Believers (*amir al-mu'minin*), which until then had been almost exclusively reserved for descendants of the Quraysh, the Arab tribe of the Prophet Muhammad. One exception, the Midrarid ruler of Sijilmasa – Muhammad ibn al-Fath, a Miknasa Berber – had proclaimed himself caliph in 953, but his claim had proved short-lived, while in the East, Hamza ibn Adharak (d. 828), a Khariji rebel in Sistan and Khorasan of *dihqan* stock, had made the same proclamation (I owe this information to Michael Cook), but neither attempt had the same relevance or impact as 'Abd al-Mu'min's.

'Abd al-Mu'min's reign (1130–1163) came into being when the Isma'ili Fatimid imamate–caliphate (909–1171) was approaching its end, and when the Sunni Abbasids (750–1258) still held Baghdad as the capital of their caliphate, but were struggling to maintain their religious and political authority over the rest of the Islamic world. 'Abd al-Mu'min's success in establishing a non-Arab caliphate – even though he would eventually legitimize his rule by claiming Arab descent – was due to a number of factors that will be explored in the following chapters. Among those factors, his personality certainly played a crucial role.

Physically he was of medium size, muscular, robust, with fair complexion and dark hair; in his advanced age he had a dignified bearing, white hair and thick beard. Pro-Almohad sources report that he was an eloquent man who was loved at first sight by everybody who met him. His teacher Ibn Tumart described him as endowed with a generous hand and a smiling face, firm in his faith and prudent in his conduct. His appearance had been predicted in verses, according to the anonymous Almohad source *Kitab al-ansab*:

> Among [the Arab Murra] a handsome man will appear, whose nature was made to bring good news.
>
> His whole mien will radiate splendour around him and his looks will be as brilliant as if water fell drop by drop.

A thirteenth-century Latin chronicle written in the Iberian Peninsula, the *Crónica latina de los reyes de Castilla*, describes 'Abd al-Mu'min as a man of discerning intelligence, generous and bellicose (*vir discretus largus et bellicosus*).

Ibn Tumart's follower, al-Baydhaq, said of 'Abd al-Mu'min's intelligence that in the time it took others to grasp one issue, he had understood ten – and he was undoubtedly an intelligent ruler, as will become evident in the following chapters. An outsider among the Masmuda, he prevailed in the difficult process of the succession of the Mahdi Ibn Tumart (d. 1130), who had never married and died without offspring. 'Abd al-Mu'min afterwards managed to successfully hold together the lands he had conquered with a powerful army and an efficient administration. This included the establishment of the *talaba*, the political-religious scholarly elite loyal to him, in order to balance the power of the Masmuda tribes that had formed the original basis of the Almohad movement. This helped him ensure the continuity of rule within his family. After executing those who had shown disaffection, 'Abd al-Mu'min managed to avoid alienating the Masmuda who constituted the Berber backbone of the Almohad army, even after incorporating into that army the Arab tribes he had defeated in the battle of Sétif, in modern-day Algeria. His economic policies were largely effective in gaining him support, and involved efficient taxation and agricultural development; the peculiarly shaped coins he minted demonstrate his acumen to convey complex religious and political messages in simple, but not simplistic, ways.

As for his generosity, 'Abd al-Mu'min knew how to reward those who helped him, and how to bestow benefits in order to gain new followers. This was especially so in al-Andalus, where the population had risen up against the previous Berber rulers, the Almoravids, and where local rulers had emerged who did not generally welcome a new military intervention from across the Strait of Gibraltar. Examples of 'Abd al-Mu'min's generosity towards Andalusis – both men and women – are many. Asma' al-'Amiriyya, a woman who claimed descent from al-Mansur ibn Abi 'Amir – the powerful chamberlain who had held effective power in tenth-century Umayyad Córdoba – wrote to him asking to be exempted from hosting his troops and from having her house and fortune confiscated. After he granted all of her requests, she composed multiple poems praising him. In Bougie, he sought out a merchant who had given him food when he was a poor student; when it turned out that he had already died, he bestowed his generosity on his family. In his dealings with the Arab tribesmen incorporated into the Almohad army, he lavishly fed them at magnificent banquets, in addition to rewarding them with booty and payments. Sharing food was a crucial activity in 'Abd al-Mu'min's way of rule, one that originated in the Berber custom of communal meals. This was only one among other existing practices that he cleverly used to support his rule and to ensure his dynastic succession. In al-Dhahabi's (d. 1348) *Ta'rikh*, the caliph is praised for his austerity: 'During his life he only wore wool (*suf*). In his audience hall (*majlis*) there were not mats, the floor was covered with just gravel and in the place where he sat there were palm leaves as the only sign of distinction.' After meeting 'Abd al-Mu'min, the Zirid prince Ibn Shaddad (d. after 1204) highlighted among his virtues his equanimity and deep religiosity.

'Abd al-Mu'min was also a great military commander, who complemented his own abilities by surrounding himself with capable men. He fought primarily against the Muslim opponents of the Almohads; although he did not engage directly in battle with the Christians in the Iberian Peninsula, he did fight against the Normans in present-day Tunisia. His secretary, the Andalusi Abu Ja'far ibn 'Atiyya, took delight in the caliphal gardens, while 'Abd al-Mu'min retorted that nothing was comparable to a military parade. Like other conquerors and builders of empires, he was not shy about resorting to violence, or even cruelty, in order to quash internal revolts and threats to his rule. The earliest non-Almohad source to mention the Almohads, the Damascene historian Ibn al-Qalanisi (d. 1160), highlighted this aspect of his reign.

In verses dedicated to 'Abd al-Mu'min, Asma' al-'Amiriyya wrote:

> We know that God's help and the clear victory belong to our lord, the Prince of the Believers...
>
> You have transmitted Ibn Tumart's knowledge, you have taught it to us and you have kept his promise intact until now.

In the above portrait of 'Abd al-Mu'min as a generous and bellicose man of discerning intelligence, his religious knowledge has received little mention, yet his career actually started when, as a young religious student, he left his village to continue his studies in the East, as many Maghribis had done before him. However, he was soon to discover that he need not travel so far: he found what he was looking for in the Maghrib, in the teachings of Ibn Tumart, whom he met in Mallala, near Bougie (in present-day Algeria). After learning Ibn Tumart's doctrines, he shaped and disseminated his tutor's works to such an extent that what we know about Ibn Tumart today has all essentially come to us through 'Abd al-Mu'min.

'Abd al-Mu'min is said to have been eloquent in Arabic, unlike most of his contemporaries, whose mother tongue was Berber. He is not credited with having authored any book of his own; only a handful of verses are attributed to him, although it is highly improbable that he actually wrote them himself. His secretaries wrote the letters he directed to the *talaba* in the main urban centres of his empire and to the rest of his subjects. He was the patron of famous scholars such as the physician Ibn Zuhr (Avenzoar) (1090–1161), and the doctor and philosopher Ibn Tufayl (d. 1185). During his reign, Ibn Rushd al-Hafid (d. 1198), known in the Latin West as Averroes, was recruited into the Almohad religious elites and started writing his commentaries on Aristotle.

The Kutubiyya mosque in Marrakesh, with its imposing minaret, was built during 'Abd al-Mu'min's reign, as was the mosque of Tinmal in the Atlas Mountains, where Ibn Tumart was buried. Pilgrimage to the grave of the Almohad Mahdi was one of several religious and political rituals that 'Abd al-Mu'min established in order to lend legitimacy to his rule, and for some time fully replaced the pilgrimage to Mecca within the lands of the empire. Jews and Christians, as well as Muslims, were also forced to convert to the Almohad understanding of Islam under 'Abd al-Mu'min's rule.

These unconventional policies highlight the fact that these were extraordinary times. Both Ibn Tumart and 'Abd al-Mu'min were considered deviant by Sunni scholars such as Ibn Taymiyya (d. 1328). The historian Ibn al-Qalanisi accused the Mahdi of contradicting the Revealed Law (*mukhalafat al-shari'a al-islamiyya*). While Almohadism is difficult to define as it evolved through time, suffice it to mention here that it involved a radical re-centring of Islam: with the appearance of the Berber Mahdi, it was as if the Hijaz – the part of the Arabian Peninsula where Mecca and Medina, the holy places of Islam, are situated – had been relocated to the Maghrib. Truth now resided there, as brought by the Mahdi Ibn Tumart, 'the heir of the station of prophecy' (*warith maqam al-nubuwwa*), and maintained by the Almohad caliph. This radical re-centring, whereby the Berbers replaced the Arabs as the chosen people, would eventually be undermined by some of the decisions taken by 'Abd al-Mu'min himself. Foremost among these was his adoption of an Arab genealogy and his incorporation of Arab tribes into the Almohad army, as well as the gradual undermining of Ibn Tumart's Mahdism through the support of reformed Malikism and philosophy, especially by 'Abd al-Mu'min's first two successors, his son Abu Ya'qub Yusuf (r. 1163–1184) and his grandson Abu Yusuf Ya'qub (r. 1184–1199).

Usually understood as a rigorist and puritanical movement, Almohadism looked to the past in order to change the present, while at the same time departing in many ways from that past, as shown by its non-Arab, Berber roots. Apart from its original Masmuda tribal basis, it found support among certain scholars who had felt alienated under Almoravid rule, who had described themselves as 'strangers' (*ghuraba'*), according to a famous *hadith*. Their input fostered a complex, vibrant and stimulating intellectual milieu that characterizes the rule of the first three Mu'minid caliphs. It was then that thinkers such as Ibn Tufayl, Averroes, Maimonides (d. 1204) and the Sufi Muhyi l-din Ibn 'Arabi (d. 1240) were active with their path-breaking intellectual output closely connected to the Almohad political, religious and educational project. The emergence under Almohad rule of these and other highly innovative thinkers, and the fact that Almohadism was presented as a *retour aux sources* while promoting breaks with standard doctrines and practices (e.g. Mahdism and impeccability; the imposition of a single creed; forced conversion; a new pilgrimage centre; the religious use of the Berber language; the abandonment of some Maliki legal practices), remind us of the difficulty of pigeonholing what the Almohads did and represented throughout their history. Yet 'Abd al-Mu'min's life opens a window to a better understanding of how it all began.

2

LOOKING FOR KNOWLEDGE: THE ENCOUNTER WITH IBN TUMART

TRAVELLING EAST IN HAMMADID TERRITORY: MALLALA AND IBN TUMART

'Abd al-Mu'min was around twenty-three years old in 1117, when in the company of his paternal uncle Ya'lu he reached the town of Mallala, near Bougie, as a student travelling to the East in pursuit of knowledge. It was there that he met Ibn Tumart.

Bougie would be conquered by 'Abd al-Mu'min some thirty years later. When he first arrived in the vibrant port town, it was the capital of the Hammadid kingdom (1015–1152). The Hammadids were a branch of the Zirids, Sanhaja Berbers who had been set up as governors of Ifriqiya by the Fatimid caliphs when in 969 they departed to Egypt, never to return. By the mid-eleventh century, after the Zirids of Qayrawan declared their independence from the Fatimids, the imam-caliphs in Cairo sent groups of Arab nomads to invade their lands. Pillaging ensued, and many urban centres such as Qayrawan suffered destruction and abandonment. The Zirids took refuge in the coastal town of al-Mahdiyya, and the Hammadids also felt more secure moving from their inland capital, Qal'at Bani Hammad, to a new maritime capital, Bougie, that prospered thanks to trade with the rest of the Islamic world and with Genoa.

'Abd al-Mu'min was born around 1094 in the village of Tajra near Nedroma, in a mountainous region of the district of Tlemcen, home to his tribe, the Zanata Kumya. Since childhood, there had been indications that an extraordinary destiny awaited him, and while a student in Tlemcen, 'Abd al-Mu'min continued to show signs of a charismatic personality. One day, when he was staying outside the town, he was informed that one of his fellow students had been imprisoned. He returned to the town and managed to set him free, as the porters and guards obeyed his orders and touched him to obtain his blessing (*baraka*).

Al-Marrakushi (d. after 1224) states that 'Abd al-Mu'min met Ibn Tumart in Fanzara, a village where he was a school teacher, but most sources place their encounter elsewhere. Ibn al-Qattan (d. after 1252) records that 'Abd al-Mu'min was studying in Tlemcen when a former fellow student informed him that a scholar specializing in the fundamentals of religion (*usul al-din*) had arrived in Bougie, prompting 'Abd al-Mu'min to travel there to meet him. According to Ibn Khaldun (d. 1406), when news reached Tlemcen that the scholar Ibn Tumart had arrived in Bougie, 'Abd al-Mu'min was assigned the task of bringing him to the town in order to replace a teacher who had just died. An earlier source, al-Baydhaq, states that 'Abd al-Mu'min's trip to Bougie was motivated by his desire to continue his studies in the East. Travel for study (*rihla fi talab al-'ilm*), usually combined with pilgrimage to Mecca, was a common practice among those from the Maghrib and al-Andalus who aspired to become scholars. Ibn Tumart, the man 'Abd al-Mu'min met in Mallala who changed his destiny, was a scholar who had already performed this *rihla*.

Born between 1078 and 1081 in Igiliz, Ibn Tumart was fourteen to seventeen years older than 'Abd al-Mu'min. His birthplace was a village in the Anti-Atlas Mountains facing the Sus Valley, situated high up on a mountainside at an altitude of 1354 m, some 60 km east of Tarudant, a location identified in 2004 by Abdallah Fili and Jean-Pierre van Staëvel (see Map 1).

Broadly speaking, Ibn Tumart belonged to the Masmuda of the Sus, the region to the south of Marrakesh between the Atlantic Ocean and the Dra' river valley, including not only the Sus river valley, but also the Atlas and Anti-Atlas Mountains. More specifically, Ibn Tumart belonged to the Harga tribe, the Arabic rendition of the Berber name

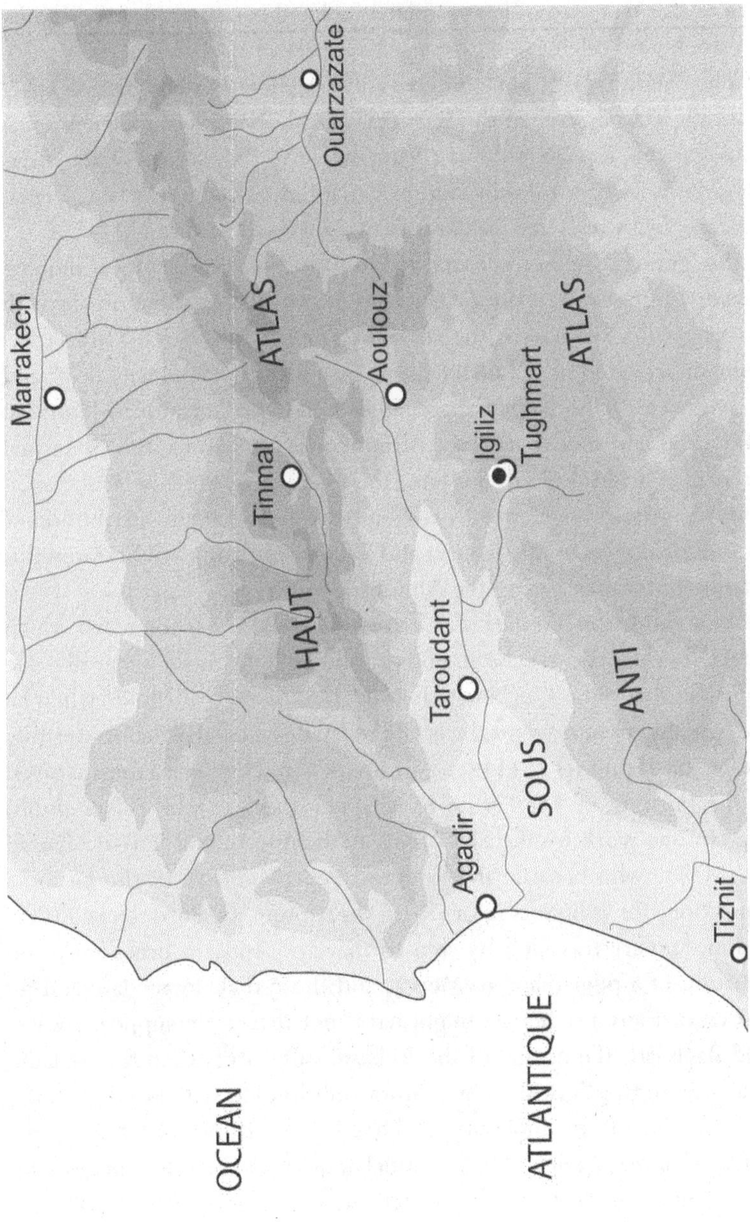

Map 1 *Igiliz (© Mission archéologique Igiliz).*

Ait Argen. This name refers to the argan tree, which is common in the area to this day, providing wood for fuel and construction, fodder for livestock, and oil.

The Masmuda tribal confederation included other tribes apart from the Harga, such as the Ragraga, Masakkala, Haha and Massagina between the Tansift and Sus rivers, while in the valleys of the Atlas Mountains there were the Gadmiwa, Ganfisa, Saktana, Hintata, Urika, Hazraja, Igalwan (Glawa), Banu Wawazgit and Haskura.

Ibn Tumart's father is described in some sources as a local notable (*amgar*), but also as a poor man who improved his situation through marriage to a woman of the Masakkala tribe. The name Tumart has been interpreted as a female name that means 'happiness, joy' and as evidence of the Berber matrilineal trends that produced feminine affiliations common among the Almoravids (Ibn Fatima, Ibn Ghaniya). According to Mehdi Ghouirgate, the eventual weight of Arabness – with its prevalent agnatism that went together with the attribution of Arab genealogies to Ibn Tumart and 'Abd al-Mu'min – obliterated this matrilineal reality among the Almohads.

As a child, Ibn Tumart was known as *asafu*, a Berber word which refers to a flaming torch, an ember, and to light more generally. He began studying the Qur'an at an early age. Around 1106–7, when he was roughly twenty-eight, he is said to have visited al-Andalus to study under Ibn Hamdin (d. 1114). This Cordoban judge was later involved in the burning of *The Revival of Religious Sciences* (*Ihya' 'ulum al-din*) – a famous work by the Shafi'i jurist, theologian and Sufi al-Ghazali (d. 1111), who became the foremost representative of the period's aspirations for religious reform – in the mosque of Córdoba in 1109.

Ibn Tumart travelled by ship to the East; most sources make no mention of a pilgrimage to Mecca, and those that do are late and do not record any teacher he might have met there. He supposedly visited Baghdad, the capital of the Abbasid caliphate, when the de facto rulers were the Turkish Seljuk emirs, and studied with scholars of the *madrasa* Nizamiyya, including al-Ghazali himself. Upon learning that his *Ihya' 'ulum al-din* had been publicly burnt, al-Ghazali expressed his desire for someone to one day exact revenge on his behalf. Ibn Tumart demanded to be charged with this task, and set off on his return to the

Maghrib. This anecdote fashions Ibn Tumart as the student of the most influential scholar of his times, thus providing him with both a scholarly genealogy and a rationale for his revolt. However, due to chronological inconsistencies, from very early on doubts were raised about this alleged encounter with al-Ghazali, for example by the Eastern historians Ibn al-Athir (d. 1233) and Ibn Khallikan (d. 1282). As in the case of Ibn Tumart's alleged visit to al-Andalus, there is no confirmation outside the Almohad sources that he ever visited Baghdad. Local biographical dictionaries of scholars that would have documented such stays had they taken place, especially given Ibn Tumart's later relevance, are silent. Today there is consensus that the encounter with al-Ghazali never took place, but was fabricated in order to rally to the Almohad cause Maghribi and Andalusi scholars who had been attracted by al-Ghazali's doctrines and had been disappointed by the Almoravid response to them.

On his way back home, Ibn Tumart stopped in Alexandria, where he met an Andalusi Maliki scholar, al-Turtushi (d. 1126), who really was a student of al-Ghazali. There, Ibn Tumart started to put into practice the Islamic precept of commanding right and forbidding wrong (*al-amr bi-l mar'ruf wa-l nahy 'an al-munkar*). As was not uncommon with other self-styled censors, his activity was not well received, and he was forced to leave Alexandria, although, according to the *Kitab al-ansab*, he had already begun to attract some followers there.

After boarding a ship headed towards Tripoli (Libya), he began to receive credit for miraculous deeds. In one version of events, Ibn Tumart reprimanded the crew and passengers for disregarding prayer and for the presence of wine on the ship. When they ignored him, he caused a storm that finally got him everyone's attention. In another version, he was thrown into the sea by the crew, but when he failed to drown, they rescued him and finally agreed to change their ways. The ship arrived in Tripoli in 1116–7, and from there Ibn Tumart proceeded to the Zirid capital al-Mahdiyya, where he again rebuked the people for drinking wine. Fearing for his life, he continued along the coast to Monastir and Tunis. There, he rebuked the locals for refusing a proper Muslim burial to a convert from Judaism. In Constantine, he explained the correct punishment for bandits and thieves. In Bougie, he attacked the way the people dressed, as well as the fact that men and women mixed during the celebrations marking the end of Ramadan. Ibn Khaldun described him as wearing a traditional Maghribi bag and carrying a stick that he sometimes used against those he rebuked. Local authorities were not pleased with the activities of 'the jurist from the Sus', as he was called. Asked who had given him permission to command what was good, his answer was that God and his Prophet had entrusted him to do so. He was then either asked to leave or decided for himself to depart out of fear for his life.

After leaving Bougie, Ibn Tumart stopped over in Mallala for several weeks. There, he was offered protection by the local Banu Uryagul; according to another version, the sons of the Hammadid emir of Bougie built a small mosque for him to teach in. The mosque was near the house of Abu Muhammad Yarzighan ibn 'Umar, whose Berber name Ibn Tumart replaced with the Arab name 'Abd al-Wahid, and who would accompany him back to Igiliz. In Mallala, where he would typically sit on a stone under a tree, Ibn Tumart devoted himself to prayer and teaching. One day, he announced the arrival of someone who would be decisive in the success of his preaching.

Before arriving in Mallala, 'Abd al-Mu'min had been having dreams he did not know how to interpret. For example, in one he was eating from the same plate as the Almoravid emir, but was so hungry that he eventually took all the food for himself. He decided to ask Ibn Tumart about the meaning of these dreams. Once in Mallala, Ibn Tumart singled him out from among the other students. When 'Abd al-Mu'min explained that he was travelling to the East in pursuit of knowledge, Ibn Tumart gave him a famous reply: 'The science that you are looking for in the Mashriq [East] you have now found in the Maghrib [West].'

'Abd al-Mu'min met in secret with Ibn Tumart, who showed him a book with a red cover that dealt with predictions (*al-jafr*), based on which Ibn Tumart concluded that 'Abd al-Mu'min would be instrumental in establishing the order (*al-amr*) that would ensure the life of the faith. He then called him 'Lamp of the Almohads'. 'Abd al-Mu'min decided to discontinue his journey to the East, attaching himself instead to Ibn Tumart until his death thirteen years later. He was not the only one to do so, as the charismatic teacher attracted

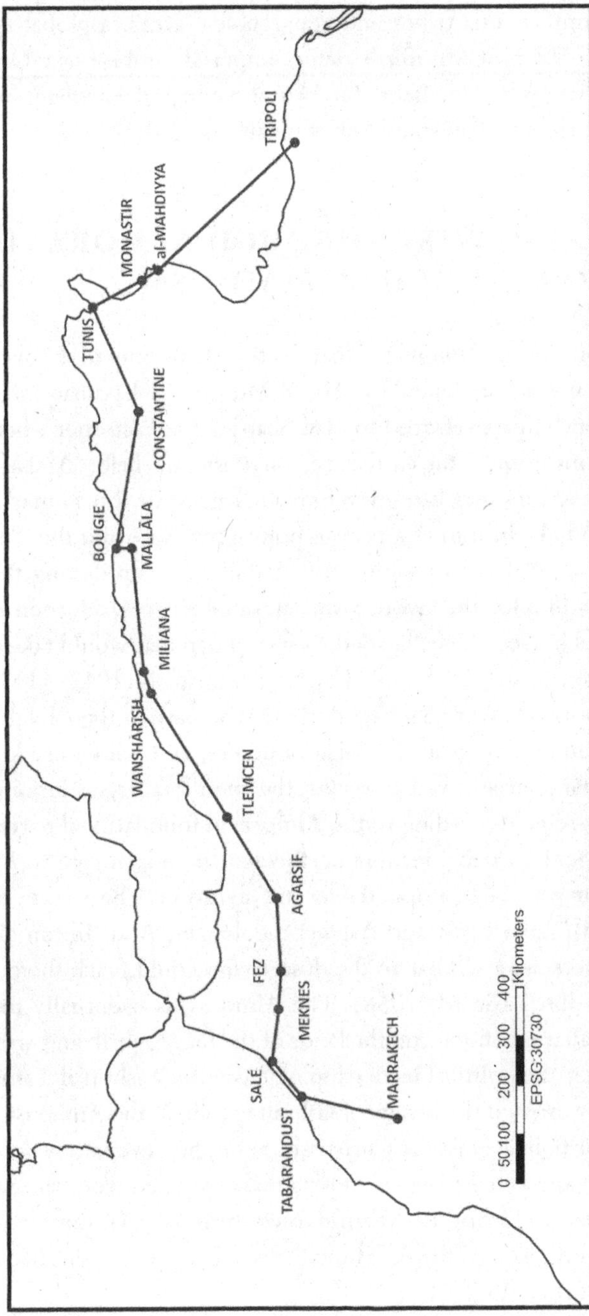

Map 2 *Ibn Tumart's itinerary from Tripoli to Marrakesh (© CCHS-CSIC; after A. Huici Miranda,* Historia política del imperio almohade, *2 vols., repr. Granada, 2000, 40–41).*

disciples from various tribes and geographical areas, a global appeal prefiguring 'Abd al-Mu'min's later imperial ambitions. One of those students was Abu Bakr ibn 'Ali al-Sanhaji al-Baydhaq, whose 'Memoirs' are our main source on this early period.

TRAVELLING WEST THROUGH ALMORAVID TERRITORY TO IGILIZ: MAHDISM

One day, Ibn Tumart announced that the time had come to depart from Mallala. He was accompanied by 'Abd al-Mu'min, al-Baydhaq and 'Abd al-Wahid ibn 'Umar, referred to as al-Sharqi, 'the Easterner', because he hailed from Ifriqiya, the eastern region of the Maghrib. 'Abd al-Wahid ibn 'Umar's mother had given him a mare, while Ibn Tumart rode a mule. 'Abd al-Mu'min at a certain point grew sore and Ibn Tumart asked 'Abd al-Wahid to let him mount the mare, predicting that he would repay him for the favour with 'elevated palaces, adorned slaves and beautiful horses'. They headed west on a trip that would take them to Marrakesh, the capital founded by the Almoravids (1042–1147).

The Almoravids were Sanhaja Berbers who earned their livelihood as nomad camel drivers in the Saharan desert, and who were known for their characteristic veil covering the men's faces, as among the modern Tuaregs. According to the Almoravid foundational narrative, a group of Sanhaja tribal leaders performed the pilgrimage to Mecca and, on their way back, stopped over in Qayrawan. There, they asked a renowned Maliki jurist and Ash'ari theologian, Abu 'Imran al-Fasi (d. 1037), to send a scholar to the desert who could teach them. The scholar was Ibn Yasin (d. 1058). The Almoravids eventually moved out of the Sahara, conquering the lands of the far Maghrib and western Algeria under the political leadership of Yusuf ibn Tashfin al-Lamtuni. In 1086 they crossed the Straits of Gibraltar to help the Andalusi Taifa kings in their fight against the Christians. Soon, however, they deposed those kings, and ruled over an empire that stretched from the Sahara to al-Andalus, and from the Atlantic to western Algeria, this being the first Berber empire and the first time the whole of al-Andalus had been subject to Berber rule.

The Almoravid emirs relied on the Maliki jurists as advisors in their policies, which were synthesized in the motto, 'Calling to the Truth, rejecting injustice and abolishing illegal taxation'. The main source of legitimization for their rule was jihad against the Iberian Christians. The Almoravids, like the Seljuk Turks in the East, lacked an ethnic link with the origins of Islam, whereas the Sunni caliphs of the time, the Abbasids, were members of the Prophet Muhammad's tribe and close relatives of the Prophet himself. In order to justify their fight as a jihad, the Almoravids were told by some Andalusi Taifa kings that they needed to acknowledge a legitimate *imam* (leader). They then paid obedience to the caliph in Baghdad as Prince of the Believers (*amir al-mu'minin*), inventing for themselves the lesser title of Prince of the Muslims (*amir al-muslimin*).

After leaving Mallala in 1117, Ibn Tumart and his students travelled through Almoravid territory. On the road to Tlemcen, Ibn Tumart renovated two mosques that had fallen into disrepair. In Wansharish, they met 'Abd Allah ibn Muhsin al-Wansharisi, nicknamed al-Bashir for his clairvoyance, who decided to join them. In Batha, they were hosted by a rich landlord, Yusuf ibn 'Abd al-'Aziz. Ibn Tumart left him a talisman made with a piece of leather from his bag, and told him to keep it for his children, as they would need it one day when a king arrived – as indeed happened when 'Abd al-Mu'min conquered the village.

In Tlemcen, Ibn Tumart stopped a wedding procession, breaking the drums and ordering the bride from the chair in which she was transported. In Agarsif, he condemned the crucifixion of a living convict, stating it was only permissible to crucify the body of a criminal after execution. By doing so, he was criticizing the practice of the Maliki legal school prevalent in North Africa and al-Andalus, and showing his preference for the Shafi'i position, which was later followed by the Almohads. He also convinced the governor to abolish illegal taxes. In Dashr Qallal, he condemned the mixing of men and women at musical gatherings, but the people replied that that was just the way things were done there. In Fez, he taught the fundamentals of religion, ordered his companions to break musical instruments and debated with the local scholars. His success led the governor to exile him, and to send a report about him to Marrakesh.

In Salé, a port town on the Atlantic coast, Ibn Tumart and his companions were hosted by a local family, the Banu 'Ashara. 'Abd al-Mu'min would later remember how he, Ibn Tumart and 'Abd al-Wahid ibn 'Umar al-Sharqi were so poor at this point that they had but one piece of bread. When they had to cross the river Bu Ragrag, they offered the bread to the boatman, but he would only accept it as fare for two of them, forcing 'Abd al-Mu'min to swim across. When he grew tired and tried to grab on to the boat, the boatman beat him away, so that only with great effort did he manage to reach the other side. Proceeding along the Atlantic coast, in Umm Rabi' they were asked to pay a toll in order to cross a bridge. Ibn Tumart, furious, refused, claiming that the road belonged to all Muslims. He spoke in Berber, as he did on other occasions, recorded by al-Baydhaq and the anonymous author of the *Kitab al-ansab*, sentences that are among the earliest testimonies of the Masmuda language.

Ibn Tumart and his students arrived in Marrakesh in the year 1120 or perhaps earlier. He publicly criticized the traditional face veil worn by Almoravid men, while Almoravid women moved about in public unveiled, including a sister of the Almoravid emir 'Ali ibn Yusuf ibn Tashfin (r. 1106–1143). Ibn Tumart entered the Friday mosque and sat in the first row near the pulpit; told that this place belonged to the emir, he answered that mosques belonged to God alone, and did not move. When the emir arrived, Ibn Tumart advised him to forbid the evil in his domain, as he was responsible for his subjects.

Ibn Tumart also taught the fundamentals of religion, debating with the local scholars in the presence of the Almoravid emir. One of these scholars was the Andalusi Malik ibn Wuhayb (d. 1131), who alerted the emir that Ibn Tumart was the man 'of the square dirham' – a reference to the peculiar shape of the Almohad dirhams later minted by 'Abd al-Mu'min. Ibn Wuhayb also warned the emir that Ibn Tumart was an innovator who would corrupt the masses, and called for him to be imprisoned. Two viziers – one of them Yintan ibn 'Umar – argued that to imprison someone who knew God so well was poor advice. Eventually, Yintan ibn 'Umar managed to convince the emir that it would be better to expel Ibn Tumart from town instead. Ibn Tumart then settled in the cemetery, and when asked why he had not left Marrakesh, answered that he was now in a land over which the emir did not rule. Ibn Tumart was keen to establish a distinction between God's territory and the ruler's sphere of control and action – paradoxically, the Almohad polity was to merge both. Eventually, Ibn Tumart and his companions left Marrakesh, moving to Aghmat Urika, where he again debated with local scholars. According to Ibn al-Qattan, it was there that Ibn Tumart broke his oath of allegiance to the Almoravids.

From Aghmat, Ibn Tumart and his companions travelled through the Atlas Mountains. In Igalwan they stayed with the Hazraja tribal leader (shaykh) Isma'il Igig. They then moved to the territory of the Hintata, where they met Abu Hafs 'Umar Inti and Yusuf ibn Wanudin. He preached to the Ganfisa and descended towards the Atlantic Ocean. Finally, in 1121 they arrived in Igiliz, Ibn Tumart's village. He had been away for fifteen years.

They settled in the so-called Ribat of the Harga. The term *ribat* refers to the activity of those who devoted themselves to a life of asceticism and renunciation but also of military engagement with external enemies or internal heretics. In the history of post-conquest North Africa, this activity had played an important role in the process of Islamization. The term can also refer to a specific place or building where such activity took place. In fact, the Almoravids (*al-murabitun*) derived their name from this term: they were those who had engaged in *ribat* life along the border with the pagan *bilad al-sudan* (the land of the blacks), and also fought against the heretical Bargawata, who followed a prophet of their own and who were located along the Atlantic coast to the south of Salé. In the case of Ibn Tumart and his followers, the enemies were the Almoravids, denounced as unbelievers.

Since 2009, a Moroccan–French team led by Ahmed S. Ettahiri, Abdallah Fili and Jean-Pierre van Staëvel have been excavating the site of the Ribat of the Harga at the summit of Jebel Igiliz. The site is a true eagle's nest, a rural mountain fortress surrounded by double walls with three gates, two of which must have been quite monumental. Similar fortresses that served as a refuge for the local population when subject to an external attack or as point of control of the surrounding territory were probably common in the region.

While it is not yet possible to ascertain how representative the ribat at Igiliz was of broader local customs, it offers important materials on the endogenous processes of state formation in tribal and rural contexts. Indeed, the excavations at Jebel Igiliz have brought to light a large settlement containing stone buildings for political, military, religious and economic purposes, as well as several dwellings. Of special interest is a command zone (*qasba*), formed by an area shaped as a nearly perfect square (the imperfection is the result of the orography of the site) inserted into a larger site, all revealing the existence of a clear hierarchy of authority and power. A small elite resided here, protected by a complex system of entrances shaped in such a way that control could be easily exercised. The hierarchical relations are inscribed in the site: the lower court of the *qasba* was a place for service and communal practices, and was subordinate to the area where the leader lived.

Also of interest are a large mosque and two smaller oratories, several cisterns for collecting water, two excavated caves and a building between the *qasba* and the large mosque that can be identified as a centre for religious teaching and a lodge for students. The whole settlement can be confidently dated to the early twelfth century, although some constructions may have been established earlier. The community of men and women who lived there were led by those who occupied the *qasba* and engaged in military as well as religious activities, as proven by the remains of numerous weapons found at the site. The presence of latrines and ablution rooms, and a material culture that includes ceramics imported from al-Andalus, point to a community that had links beyond the local setting. The information provided by the literary sources matches up well with what has been found: a base from which to wage jihad against the Almoravids and a centre for the indoctrination and spread of Ibn Tumart's teachings within a tribal milieu.

Retiring to a cave for a time in order to seek purification and obtain *baraka* (blessings) was common in Berber lands; the Prophet Muhammad himself had retired to a cave in Mount Hira, where he first received God's revelation. At Jebel Igiliz, Ibn Tumart confined himself for an unspecified period in one such cave (*ghar*). The local people used to visit him at the beginning of the day to seek his *baraka*. Ibn Tumart stroked their heads with his hand and invoked God in their favour. The fourteenth-century chronicle *al-Hulal al-mawshiyya* describes Ibn Tumart's teachings:

> The first thing [Ibn Tumart] did upon taking command was to write them a book in the Berber language which he called *al-tawhid*. It was divided into seven parts according to the seven days of the week, and he ordered them to read a section each day after the morning prayer after finishing the selection from the Koran. In it, there was the knowledge of God and the other dogmas, such as the knowledge of God's decrees, and predestination, and faith in what is characteristic of God, and of what is impossible in Him and what is possible, and what a Muslim should do to impose orthodoxy and prohibit the illicit and to join together in brotherhood for this purpose.
>
> (Translation by Madeleine Fletcher, 1991)

Manuscript arab. 1451, preserved at the National Library of France, contains the *Kitab* (book) attributed to Ibn Tumart, and records that it was dictated in the year 1121 at the Ribat of the Harga. It contains a section on the Mahdi, which essentially explains that falsehood can only be vanquished by the Mahdi and truth can only be established and maintained by the Mahdi because of his 'impeccability' (*'isma*). Belief in the Mahdi is obligatory and to doubt him is unbelief. The Prophet Muhammad had put an end to ignorance, but innovations and discrepancies had reappeared after the rule of the Rightly Guided Caliphs that succeeded him. The Mahdi would restore truth, filling the earth with justice just as now it was filled with iniquity; his rule would last until the Final Hour. Ibn Tumart also taught that the Almoravids had to be combatted, as they had departed from the truth through their corrupt practices and their anthropomorphic beliefs. According to most sources, it was in Igiliz that Ibn Tumart was acknowledged as being the Mahdi and the impeccable *imam* (leader).

During his stay at Igiliz, Ibn Tumart held a communal banquet (*asmas*) and put salt in the food, claiming: 'This is the pact [*'ahd*] of God and his Prophet between us and you according to the Qur'an and

Sunna.' He then started to eat to prove that he was a man like everybody else and that prophets also ate. The contractual aspect of this episode is evident: the Mahdi was using a pre-existing tribal practice – the communal banquet – to bind his followers to him and his cause. On this particular occasion, Ibn Tumart predicted that the Almoravids would be defeated and lose their horses. He ordered his tribesmen to build an enclosure (*asarag*) to keep these plundered steeds, as Igiliz would soon become a military base.

In 1122, the Almoravid governor of the Sus sent one of his delegates against the Banu Wartatik of the Harga. They were taken captive and imprisoned in Tiwanwin, the capital of the Sus. Shortly afterwards, the Harga inflicted a defeat on the Almoravids, who had attacked them at Igiliz, taking prisoners and horses, just as Ibn Tumart had predicted. Fearing another Almoravid attack, Ibn Tumart ordered cisterns to be built to collect water in case of a siege. He also offered to leave so that his tribesmen would not suffer, but the Harga maintained their support for him.

Some of Ibn Tumart's followers travelled to the neighbouring Atlas Mountains to rally the local tribes to his cause. In 1123, the Almoravid emir, after returning from al-Andalus, sent in troops to besiege Igiliz. Ibn Tumart directed the defence, reminding the Harga of the booty they would gain if victorious. They were on the verge of being defeated when they heard the drums of the Hintata, who were coming to their aid. The Almoravids were defeated, while the Harga tribesmen who were held prisoner in Tiwanwin escaped and joined the Mahdi. That same year saw further military engagements with the Almoravids, the outcome of which is difficult to discern.

Ibn Tumart and his companions resided at Igiliz for three years, from 1121–2 to 1124–5, when they left for Tinmal in the Atlas Mountains at the invitation of the Hazmira tribe, who had joined Ibn Tumart's cause, perhaps because Igiliz was not considered safe enough. Little is known about the fate of Igiliz after their departure. Jebel Igiliz and especially the cave remained a place of local veneration, but the move to Tinmal relegated it to a marginal position in Almohad memory.

TRAVELLING NORTH: TINMAL AND THE PURGES

On the road to Tinmal, the Ganfisa pledged obedience to Ibn Tumart. Tinmal was an impregnable fortress on the upper part of the Nafis river in the High Atlas Mountains, some 100 km south of Marrakesh. We do not know how many of Ibn Tumart's followers accompanied him on this 'emigration' similar to the Prophet Muhammad's flight from Mecca to Medina. However, the events that ensued shortly after they settled in Tinmal indicate that they must have been relatively numerous. Every day, Ibn Tumart went to the open-air oratory (*shari'a*), sat on a square stone and taught his doctrines to the inhabitants of Tinmal. The Hazmira who attended these sessions carried weapons, which made Ibn Tumart fear for his life. Eventually, they were massacred, the first of other purges to follow. Fifteen thousand men are said to have been killed, their families taken captive and their possessions distributed among the Almohads. Only those loyal to Ibn Tumart were allowed to live in Tinmal, whose population was now made up of an array of groups from various tribes and geographical locations that came to be referred to as *ahl Tinmal*, or 'People of Tinmal'.

Ibn Tumart reinforced the fortress's natural defences during the year 1126. He also consolidated his control of the mountains to the south and west of Marrakesh. The Gadmiwa joined the movement, while the Haskura would hesitate until the conquest of Marrakesh. The Almoravids were at the time tied down in al-Andalus, trying to stop the Christian military advance. Alfonso the Battler, king of Aragon (r. 1104–1134), had launched a campaign inside al-Andalus that reached all the way to the sea in Algeciras, with the help of some Andalusi Christian communities. The Cordoban Maliki jurist Ibn Rushd al-Jadd (d. 1126), Averroes' grandfather, travelled to Marrakesh to discuss the deportation of these communities to the Maghrib with the emir, and during his visit he recommended building walls to protect Marrakesh from the Almohads. It was probably then that a number of fortresses were also built to stop the Almohads from descending into the plain of Marrakesh. This was an effective move that did manage to halt them for a time. In 1127, Ibn Tumart led a campaign in the Sus. Later, a group of the Haskura killed the Almohad instructor sent to them, and in 1128 were in turn attacked and massacred; during the fighting Ibn Tumart received a head injury.

As its followers increased in number, the movement acquired a more defined political and military organization, to be discussed in Chapter 4. The Council of Ten (*al-jama'a*) was formed by the first disciples of Ibn Tumart, including 'Abd al-Mu'min and al-Bashir al-Wansharisi. The tribal leaders (shaykhs) of the Harga, Hintata, Gadmiwa and Ganfisa formed the Council of Fifty. In the year 1129, according to al-Baydhaq (1125 according to other authors), while the Almoravids were too engaged in al-Andalus to pay close attention to the Almohads, a purge (*tamyiz*) was carried out among the tribes that had joined Ibn Tumart. His disciple al-Bashir al-Wansharisi would fall into a lethargic sleep, and in this state acquired the power of distinguishing between true and false believers, a gift used to guide the purge. Only one among Ibn Tumart's early students voiced his opposition – an unnamed jurist from Ifriqiya who was consequently executed.

Shortly after the *tamyiz*, probably in order to deflect the tensions and resentment among the Almohads that ensued, an attack against Marrakesh was organized. This was a risky decision: until then, the Almohads had confronted the Almoravids in the mountains where they had the advantage; now they were moving to the plains, where the Almoravids moved with ease. The military campaign was headed by al-Bashir al-Wansharisi. A first encounter outside the walls of Marrakesh proved promising for the Almohads, who decided to camp in the al-Buhayra orchard. The ensuing siege lasted some six weeks. A battle took place in April or May 1130 in which the Almohads suffered many losses. Abu Hafs 'Umar Inti was seriously injured, and another five members of the Council of Ten died on that day. Al-Bashir al-Wansharisi's body was never found. He was said to have disappeared into the red dust; Ibn al-Qattan suggests that he was taken up to the sky, while according to some, he was buried secretly by 'Abd al-Mu'min. The French historian Évariste Lévi-Provençal was convinced that he was killed by his enemies among the Almohads for his role in the *tamyiz*.

During the siege of Marrakesh, Ibn Tumart voiced particular concerns for 'Abd al-Mu'min's safety. Having been informed that he was alive but injured in his right thigh, he said: '*qad baqiya l-amr*' ('the order remains'), indicating that 'Abd al-Mu'min was destined to succeed him, as *al-amr* was the term used to refer to the Almohad order.

The defeated Almohads returned to Tinmal divided into two groups: one led by 'Abd al-Mu'min, the other by 'Abd Allah ibn Ya'la, known as Ibn Malwiya. Seventeen years would pass before the Almohads dared another attack on Marrakesh. The Almoravids later attempted to attack Tinmal but were unsuccessful.

IBN TUMART'S DEATH AND 'ABD AL-MU'MIN'S SUCCESSION

Ibn Tumart died three months after the battle of al-Buhayra, in Ramadan (August) 1130. The Mahdi had taken ill suddenly and called the Almohads together to preach to them, announcing: 'I am leaving for a long journey.' He was buried secretly in his house.

Ibn Tumart's death was kept secret for three years, a period called *ghayba* – the same term used by Shi'is to refer to the occultation of their imams. According to al-Baydhaq, 'Abd al-Mu'min – who was by now in his fifties – was proclaimed successor in 1133, while Ibn al-Qattan gives the date as 1135. An assembly of all the loyal tribes, with women also in attendance, was convened in Tinmal. 'Abd al-Mu'min preached and asked if the pact that they had sealed with the Mahdi still stood. They answered that it did. After sermons by two members of the Council of Ten, Isma'il Igig and 'Umar Asnag, along with the tribal leaders, Ibn Tumart's death was announced. When people broke into tears, 'Abd al-Mu'min ordered them to stop. He then extended his hand and everyone paraded in front of him pledging obedience, in a ceremony that lasted three days.

'Abd al-Mu'min's succession to the Mahdi was not easy, as shown by the existence of divergent narratives on the course of events. Most sources state that Ibn Tumart had made it clear in various ways that 'Abd al-Mu'min was his choice: he was given the privilege of riding a black horse and named to lead the prayers – in the same way that Abu Bakr was considered to be the successor intended by the

Prophet Muhammad because he had named him his substitute in this same capacity. A late source, al-Zarkashi, states that the successor first acknowledged by the Council of Ten was 'Umar Asnag (from the Sanhaja), but he rejected the offer, claiming that Ibn Tumart had chosen 'Abd al-Mu'min for the role. Ibn Tumart's preference for 'Abd al-Mu'min is a recurring theme in al-Baydhaq's 'Memoirs'. This work alleges that it was known that 'Abd al-Mu'min was destined to have a glorious future even before he was born. When his mother Ta'lu was pregnant with him, she dreamt that fire came out of her and dispersed towards the four cardinal points. A diviner from Tlemcen explained that her son would one day rule over territories situated to the north, south, west and east. Another day she went with her husband to a field and fell asleep, and two swarms of bees hovered over her. When 'Abd al-Mu'min was born, she went to the same field, put her son down to join the harvest and he fell asleep. A great number of bees hovered over him without harming him, then flew away in two groups, one towards the west, the other towards the east.

However, for the pro-Marinid historian Ibn Abi Zar' (d. between 1310 and 1320), a trick was instrumental in the choice of 'Abd al-Mu'min. While the Council of Ten was deliberating, two extraordinary things happened. First, a man who owned a bird whistled and the bird said: 'Victory, conquest and power for our lord the caliph, the Prince of the Believers, 'Abd al-Mu'min.' Then a guard released a lion; everybody fled in terror, except for 'Abd al-Mu'min, who did not move in his seat. When the lion approached him, he extended his hand, calmed the animal and made it obey his orders. The Council then unanimously decided to elect 'Abd al-Mu'min as the worthiest successor to Ibn Tumart because of these seemingly miraculous deeds, without knowing they had been a calculated ruse: 'Abd al-Mu'min had secretly acquired the bird and the lion, and had trained the first to speak those words and the second to obey him.

We can only speculate about what exactly sealed 'Abd al-Mu'min's place as Ibn Tumart's successor. Ibn Tumart had left no offspring – his chastity can be contrasted with the many marriages of Ibn Yasin, the religious authority at the origins of the Almoravid movement. Ibn Tumart's brothers do not seem to have been considered for succession, perhaps because they lacked the scholarly training that Ibn Tumart and the members of the Council of Ten possessed. They may also have stayed on at Igiliz, so that when Ibn Tumart died in Tinmal they could not have any say in his succession. During the battle of al-Buhayra, five of the members of the Council of Ten had died and Abu Hafs 'Umar Inti had been seriously wounded. One of those who died was al-Bashir al-Wansharisi, Ibn Tumart's companion who was endowed with charismatic powers and probably was the 'heir apparent' of the Mahdi. His disappearance and the death of the other four eliminated many possible competitors. New members were chosen for the Council, but they would have been younger in age or more recent disciples, and thus would have had less influence.

The decimation of the Council of the Ten thus made it easier for 'Abd al-Mu'min to reach a position of pre-eminence. Modern scholars such as Évariste Lévi-Provençal and Constant Hamès have seen in his election a not unusual move in tribal milieus: that of electing an outsider as someone capable – precisely because of his foreignness – of maintaining unity among the tribal core of the movement, as he would not bring with him any legacy of internecine hatred or hostility. Tensions, however, could not be avoided, as shown by the fact that when 'Abd al-Mu'min's nomination was made public, another of Ibn Tumart's companions and a fellow member of the Council of Ten, Ibn Malwiya, defected to the Almoravids.

HISTORY, LEGEND AND ANTHROPOLOGY

We have seen how the pro-Marinid historian Ibn Abi Zar' presented 'Abd al-Mu'min's succession as the result of trickery. Pro-Almohad sources are hagiographical, while anti-Almohad sources tend to cast a negative light on both Ibn Tumart and 'Abd al-Mu'min. Both types of sources mix historical and legendary elements, with the Spanish historian Ambrosio Huici Miranda offering the most comprehensive overview.

The lack of a diverse body of contemporary sources makes it difficult to establish the historicity of certain episodes. The intent to model Ibn Tumart's figure on that of the Prophet Muhammad was identified early on, and some examples have already been mentioned. Ibn Tumart's tribe, the Harga, are referred to as Ansar (defenders), which was the name used to refer to Muhammad's supporters in Medina. The difference here is related to the fact that the attribution of an Arab genealogy to Ibn Tumart prevented a mechanical transfer from Muhammad's trajectory: if Ibn Tumart's 'real' tribe was the Arab Quraysh – as it had to be, given that the Mahdi is necessarily a descendant of the Prophet Muhammad – then the Harga had to be cast as something else, and thus were likened to those who helped the Prophet after the Hijra. The Prophetic model also resonates in some of the stories told about 'Abd al-Mu'min. The Almohad shaykh Isma'il Igig al-Hazraji offered to sit in for 'Abd al-Mu'min in his bed ahead of a planned night-time attack against him, and ended up dying as a result of his injuries, a story that directly evokes that of 'Ali risking his life to keep Muhammad's migration to Medina secret by occupying the Prophet's bed.

Other such trends can be discerned even in seemingly neutral narratives, such as that of the places visited by Ibn Tumart in his travels through North Africa from Tripoli to Marrakesh as described by al-Baydhaq (see Map 2). Upon closer inspection, the itinerary can be read as the back projection in reverse of 'Abd al-Mu'min's conquests (to be examined in the next chapter) leading to the establishment of the Almohad empire. His conquests were thus given legitimacy: the places taken by the Almohads had been visited previously by the Mahdi, who had warned their inhabitants about their wicked ways. Take, for instance, Ibn Tumart's rebuke of the people of Tunis for refusing the convert from Judaism a proper Muslim burial. Did al-Baydhaq include this episode in his 'Memoirs' to address the consequences of 'Abd al-Mu'min's forced conversion of the Jews, which led many Muslims to doubt the sincerity of the new converts' faith? Does the anecdote aim to offer a precedent from the Mahdi to guide the Almohads in their dealings with the converted Jews, or does it reveal an effort fabricated after the fact to ease the converts' transition, using the figure of the Mahdi as justification? In fact, al-Baydhaq's 'Memoirs', which allegedly offer us the personal and direct testimony of one of Ibn Tumart's followers who accompanied him from Tripoli to Igiliz, were written in order to strengthen 'Abd al-Mu'min's legitimacy as a ruler, an aim through which many episodes seem to have been filtered.

Al-Bashir al-Wansharisi was clearly a more important figure in the early stages of the Almohad movement than 'Abd al-Mu'min, but this relevance was greatly mitigated by al-Baydhaq, who tends to cast him as a trickster. For example, in the 'Memoirs' we find al-Bashir initially pretending to be illiterate, and even drooling in an effort to feign intellectual disability. Later, he attended the morning prayer well dressed and perfumed, and revealed that an angel had visited him, purified his heart and taught him the Qur'an, the Maliki text *al-Muwatta'* and other works, as he proved when examined by the Mahdi. In this way, he established his reputation as someone in contact with the Divinity. In anti-Almohad sources, acts of deceit are attributed to the Mahdi himself. For instance, he had several living men buried, leaving a hole through which they could speak. He interrogated them as if they were Almohads who had died performing jihad, and they answered describing the rewards they had obtained, in order to strengthen the fighting morale of the Almohads. Once the performance was over, Ibn Tumart had them buried alive, this time for good. Interestingly, this story gave rise in Christian writings to a similar legend told about the Prophet Muhammad, as shown by the historian Gerard Salinger.

Some of the stories told about Ibn Tumart and 'Abd al-Mu'min can be read together with those told about contemporary saintly figures – as recorded, for example, by al-Tamimi (d. 1203) and al-Tadili (d. 1229) – to reconstruct how charisma manifested itself in the tribal context in which they moved, and thus to better understand how such figures succeeded in attracting support and mobilizing men. The tribal context is often explained according to the concept of segmentarity, a social organization found mostly in rural areas characterized by the lack of centralized government and where individuals find protection in the group formed by their relatives. This group, made of different segments, is conceived as descending from a common ancestor, a belief that binds them together with the obligation to avenge wrongs done to any of them by external groups while fighting with each other over local resources. Fighting was an inherent element in tribal life and this made the tribes a reservoir of soldiers. The mobilization of tribes was facilitated by the promise of booty but most forcefully when cohesion was reached by rallying them to a cause promoted by a charismatic leader. Segmentarity, as well as Ibn Khaldun's conceptions of tribes and state formation, looms large in extant studies on the rise of the Almohads (Madeleine Fletcher, Michael Brett, Allen J. Fromherz). On the other hand, in what seems to be an unavoidable circularity, the trajectories of Ibn Tumart and 'Abd al-Mu'min have provided material for those interested in the political, social and religious history of North Africa in the past and in the present. Thus, we can easily recognize them in Ibn Khaldun's writings, but also in the much more recent model formulated by Ernst Gellner of the urban preacher who rejects established political power and takes his message to militant tribes, denouncing ungodly government in the name of sacred law.

3

FROM THE MOUNTAINS TO EMPIRE: SUBMISSION TO THE ALMOHAD CAUSE (*AL-TAWHID*) THROUGH JIHAD

DISCREDITING AND FIGHTING THE ALMORAVIDS

Almoravid rule was demonized by the Almohads: wine was sold publicly, pigs ran loose in the streets, the properties of orphans and pious foundations were dilapidated, and many other evils, both religious and legal, abounded. It is more difficult to find information about political, social and economic grievances that may have fostered the Masmuda's insurgency against the Almoravids in these sources. Almost the only example is the story of the 'blond children'.

After settling in Tinmal, Ibn Tumart feared that the Almoravids might bribe the local people into attacking the Almohads, until he realized that they, too, had reasons to be hostile toward the Almoravids. What he noticed was that many of the children had fair hair and blue eyes, even though their parents were dark-haired. The explanation given was that each year, Frankish and Christian slaves of the Almoravid emir came to collect the taxes (*kharaj*), and were lodged in the locals' houses, turning the men out and getting the women pregnant. Ibn Tumart harshly criticized the mountain people for allowing such a thing to happen, and when they retorted that they were not strong enough to oppose it, he incited them to rebel. In Ibn al-Qattan's version of this story, the Zanata – who were numerous in the army as the Almoravids had overrun various Zanata kingdoms – are the ones presented as taking advantage of the Masmuda. Senén García has analyzed how Ibn Tumart's activities in the Atlas Mountains led to an Almoravid blockade, with the construction of fortresses that dislocated the Masmuda economic networks. This threatened to destroy the mountain people's main source of income, their herds, as it prevented their seasonal migration. This dislocation eventually made it easier to rally more tribes to the Almohad cause.

The fight against the Almoravids was couched in theological terms. When in Marrakesh, Ibn Tumart had confronted the Almoravid emir, reproaching him for the sins that proliferated under his reign, and reminding him of his duty to put an end to them. The Almohads' main accusation was anthropomorphism, though modern scholars such as Delfina Serrano have shown that the accusation does not reflect the variety of doctrinal positions in the territories under Almoravid rule, and thus cannot be taken at face value as an accurate account of what the Almoravids stood for. The main aim of Ibn Tumart's accusation, rather, was to cast the Almoravids as unbelievers, making it lawful to wage jihad against them: they could be killed, their families enslaved and their goods plundered. In other words, the accusation legitimized the rebellion against those in power, to whom, according to Islamic law, obedience was due. As we shall see, it also provided a justification for eliminating the existing religious establishment and substituting it with a new one directly dependent on the Almohad ruler.

Almohad propaganda against the Almoravids demonized them as infidels, renegades, perverts and hypocrites, as a people of Satan who had destroyed the faith, done away with the Tradition of the Prophet, and enslaved their brethren, as Ibn Tumart claimed in one letter attributed to him. The Almoravids were compared to local birds, the *zarajina*, whose wings were white but chest and hearts black. The Almoravids' white wings were their defence of al-Andalus against the Christians, in recognition of which 'Abd al-Mu'min would reward the soldiers who had secured victory at the battle of Uclés in the year 1108. Otherwise, their true nature was black. Such binary oppositions are abundant in Ibn Tumart's *Kitab* and Ibn Sahib al-salat's (d. after 1197) chronicle.

The Almoravids reacted against the Almohads by calling them Kharijis, that is, likening them to the Arab tribesmen who had rebelled against the caliphs in early Islam and become famous for their bloody pursuit of an uncompromising stance on belief. In one of the letters attributed to Ibn Tumart, Almoravid criticism against him and his followers is quoted in order to rebut it. We thus learn that the Almoravids claimed that the Mahdi declared believers unbelievers just because they had sinned. Likewise, they alleged that he had condoned illicit practices. An example of this is that he allowed women who had been divorced three times to remarry their husbands (the Malikis held that a woman had to marry another man before being allowed to remarry her previous husband). The Almoravids likewise held that Ibn Tumart rejected the doctrines of the religious scholars and their consensus, and refused to obey the emir as established in Islamic law, making him a rebel.

THE LONG ROAD TO MARRAKESH, THE REBELLION OF AL-MASSI AND THE GREAT PURGE

In 1131–2, 'Abd al-Mu'min used extreme violence to put down the Hazraja and the Haskura in the eastern region of the Atlas. After being proclaimed the Mahdi's successor in 1133, he led a successful expedition to the Dra', taking the fortress of Tazagurt. The Ganfisa then killed Ibn Malwiya, the member of the Council of Ten who had defected after opposing 'Abd al-Mu'min's succession, and brought his body back to Tinmal, where it was crucified.

In 1134, 'Abd al-Mu'min took control of Tarudant and Igli in the Sus valley, where he confronted the Christian troops serving the Almoravids and burnt the fields of sugar cane. He also attacked the Banu Igaz, a tribe from the region between the Sus and the Dra', who had murdered a companion of Ibn Tumart while he was preaching to them. They responded by sending camels bearing bundles of flaming sticks into the Almohad camp; Banu Igaz tribesmen followed and managed to destroy 'Abd al-Mu'min's tents with their spears. 'Abd al-Mu'min, however, had decided to sleep elsewhere that night. From that day onwards, special troops (*al-saqa*) protected the tent where he slept. In 1135–6, he attacked the Sus again, defeating Sir ibn 'Ali, the heir apparent of the Almoravid emir, and in 1137–8 he once more confronted the Almoravids, some of whose Zanata troops defected to his side.

The Almohads had until then limited their movements to the mountains. Now, as the winter was approaching, they retreated to their fortresses. Sir ibn 'Ali died and Tashfin ibn 'Ali was proclaimed the new heir apparent and given the command of the Almoravid army. He had the help of the Christian troops led by Reverter, a Catalan viscount who, deprived of his lands by a rival, had joined the Almoravids and played an important role in their fight against the Almohads. His son 'Ali ibn Reverter would later join the Almohads and help them conquer Mallorca in 1202.

The so-called seven-year campaign was then launched (1139–1146) (see Map 3). 'Abd al-Mu'min first directed his attention towards the coastal region where the Haha tribe had joined the Almohads but showed a tendency to abandon *al-tawhid*. The Almoravid Gazula also joined the Almohads, and by 1140–1, 'Abd al-Mu'min had managed to take control of the Sus. Al-Filaki, a Sevillan bandit who had joined the Almoravid army, converted to *al-tawhid* and brought 500 captive Almoravid women with him to Tinmal.

Ten years had passed since Ibn Tumart's death. Having established control of the Sus, 'Abd al-Mu'min knew the difficulties of attempting to conquer Marrakesh from the High Atlas. He decided to go north to attack Marrakesh from both the mountains and the plains, rallying the Masmuda Gumara in the Rif mountains and his own tribe, the Kumya, in the area of Tlemcen. He named as governor of Tinmal a member of the Council of Fifty, Abu Imran Musa ibn Sulayman al-Darir, from the *ahl Tinmal*, whose daughter he had married, and marched off to the east of Marrakesh with Tashfin ibn 'Ali following him closely. Still avoiding the plains, 'Abd al-Mu'min crossed the Middle Atlas. From February to August 1141, the regions of Tadla and the Fazaz

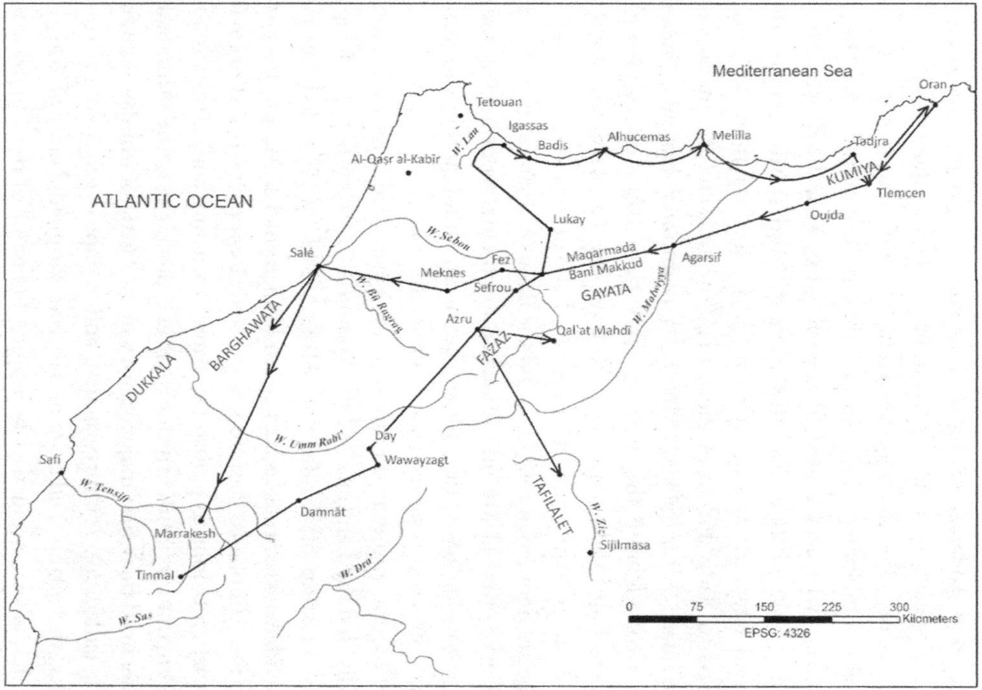

Map 3 *The campaign of 'seven years' (© CCHS-CSIC; after Rachid Bourouiba,* 'Abd al-Mu'min, flambeau des Almohades, *Algiers, 1974, 30).*

on the Atlantic side of the Middle Atlas, and Garis, Todga and the Ziz and Muluya valleys on the other side all fell under Almohad control, and new troops attracted by the prospect of booty were added to the Almohad army. The Almoravids' inability to stop 'Abd al-Mu'min's advance was partly due to the difficult situation they were facing at the time in al-Andalus, having to deal with the Christians as well as Andalusi opposition. Still, the Almohads failed to take Fez, as the winter's heavy rains flooded the rivers, forcing them to retreat into the nearby mountains. In the spring, they moved to the territory of the Gumara who had joined *al-tawhid*. Near Ksar El-Kbir, 'Umar Asnag died. When they reached the coast, 'Abd al-Mu'min saw the Almoravid navy out at sea, commanded by Ibn Maymun. In 1142, he moved to Badis and from there to Alhucemas and the mountains of Tensaman. After sacking Melilla, a communal banquet (*asmas*) was held to celebrate the marriage of various Almohad commanders – including 'Abd al-Mu'min – to local women. From there they marched on to Nedroma and Tajra, 'Abd al-Mu'min's native village. His tribesmen joined *al-tawhid*, as did the Banu Wamannu. In 1142–3, from Tajra, 'Abd al-Mu'min launched simultaneous attacks against the neighbouring areas, threatening Tlemcen, although the Almohads were not yet strong enough to attack the city itself.

In 1143, the Almoravid emir 'Ali ibn Yusuf died. His succession, which divided the Lamtuna and the Masufa – the latter being unhappy with the election of Tashfin ibn 'Ali (r. 1143–1145) – led various Almoravid shaykhs, such as Barraz ibn Muhammad al-Masufi, to cross over to the Almohads. Tashfin ibn 'Ali sent Reverter with Almoravid and Christian troops to punish the Banu Wamannu and, after a number of encounters with varying degrees of success, the Almohads finally secured their first major victory in the battle of Mindas. Tashfin ibn 'Ali called for reinforcements, and troops were sent in from Sijilmasa, al-Andalus, and from his ally the Hammadid emir of Bougie. Just as the balance seemed to be tipping in favour of the Almoravids, Reverter was killed in battle. 'Abd al-Mu'min then laid siege to Tlemcen. Tashfin ibn 'Ali retreated to Oran to await naval reinforcements from al-Andalus, while some of the Almoravid tribal leaders abandoned him. Local tribes continued to defect to the Almohad side, and in February 1145 Tashfin ibn 'Ali was killed during the Almohad assault on Oran.

When news of the fall of Oran reached Tlemcen, the Lamtuna troops headed by Ibn al-Sahrawiyya, a grandson of Yusuf ibn Tashfin, fled towards Fez. 'Abd al-Mu'min captured Tagrart, the Almoravid section of Tlemcen, killing or enslaving those of its Lamtuna inhabitants who had not already fled to Fez, despite the fact that the inhabitants had asked for peace (*aman*). The old part of the town, Agadir, endured a year-long siege before falling in 1146, leaving the Central Maghrib in the hands of the Almohads.

'Abd al-Mu'min had left Tlemcen before the town was taken, heading towards Fez. The Almoravids' internal divisions and their problems in al-Andalus favoured the Almohads, whose troops now included fighters skilled at taking walled cities. Emboldened, they laid siege to Fez, where the Almoravids had taken refuge. As he had done in Tlemcen, 'Abd al-Mu'min left before the city was taken in order to capture Meknes. In Fez, Ibn al-Sahrawiyya lost the support of the Andalusi in charge of the town's government, 'Abd Allah ibn Khiyar al-Jayyani, who decided to let the Almohads march into the city. While al-Jayyani was rewarded with a high-ranking post, Ibn al-Sahrawiyya was forced to seek refuge in al-Andalus. Other Almoravid commanders were taken captive and eventually executed, with the exception of 'Umar, a son of Yintan ibn 'Umar who had protected the Mahdi during his stay in Marrakesh.

In May 1146 Salé was taken; there 'Abd al-Mu'min met again with Ibn 'Ashara, who had hosted the Mahdi and his companions, and celebrated the Festival of Sacrifice. He then left to lay siege to Marrakesh and, towards the end of 1146, Meknes was taken. Qadi 'Iyad surrendered the town of Ceuta to the Almohads. Later, in 1147–8, the inhabitants of Ceuta killed the Almohad governor, taking advantage of the rebellion of al-Massi and the Almoravid attempt to regain power, before being forced to submit once again to Almohad rule.

Marrakesh was taken in 1147. In June 1146, 'Abd al-Mu'min had set up camp with his red tent at Guelliz, the hilltop outside the Almoravid capital. The new emir, Ishaq ibn 'Ali (r. 1145–1147), who was only sixteen, managed to defend it for nine months. Famine raged in the city because of the influx of refugees together with the Almohad blockade on provisions. According to some sources, the Christian troops opened the town to the Almohads after having negotiated the *aman* (peace). Fannu, the daughter of 'Umar ibn Yintan, led the fight against the Almohads dressed like a man and was eventually killed. The emir and many other Almoravid commanders were taken prisoner and executed. 'Abd al-Mu'min is said to have tried to save the life of the young Almoravid emir but was opposed by the tribal shaykhs, who had the upper hand. For three days, Almoravid men were killed, booty was taken and women were enslaved, with the exception of Zaynab, the daughter of Yusuf ibn Tashfin, because her husband Yahya ibn Ishaq al-Masufi, known as Wanzamar, had defected to the Almohads. Ibn Tumart's brothers took two of 'Ali ibn Yusuf's daughters. At this time, or perhaps earlier, 'Abd al-Mu'min began to use the title of caliph.

After seventeen years of constant fighting since Ibn Tumart's death, Marrakesh had been conquered and the Almohads had extended their control to the whole of the Maghrib al-Aqsa and the western part of Algeria. Soon, however, they were confronted with internal rebellions and tensions. The most dangerous was the rebellion of a man from Salé, Ibn Hud, who became known as al-Massi, as his followers came from the inhabitants of and visitors to the *ribat* of Massa, in the coastal region of the Sus valley, where he launched his rebellion. He was also called al-Hadi, rivalling the Mahdi of the Masmuda, and he managed to attract the Haha, Ragraga, Hazmira, Haskura of the plains, Dukkala and the Banu Uryagul, successfully fending off the Almohad army sent against him. Ceuta and Tangiers also rebelled, and Ibn al-Sahrawiyya returned from al-Andalus to recover the lands lost by the Almoravids, with the support of the Almoravid Banu Ghaniya who still held parts of the Iberian Peninsula. Sijilmasa and the valley of the Dra' also joined the rebels.

'Abd al-Mu'min gathered together all the original Almohad tribes, plus the former Christian mercenaries of the Almoravids, and placed them under the command of Abu Hafs 'Umar Inti. Al-Massi offered strong resistance but was eventually defeated and killed in May 1148. His body was crucified at the Bab al-Shari'a of Marrakesh. Over the following months, Abu Hafs 'Umar Inti subdued the other tribes that had joined al-Massi.

In the meantime, Ibn al-Sahrawiyya moved to Tangiers and from there to Salé. The Bargawata joined him, as did the Dukkala, Ragraga and Haha. As he posed an increasingly pressing threat, 'Abd al-Mu'min gathered a powerful army under his command to attack him. He defeated the Dukkala, and Ibn al-Sahrawiyya fled towards the Sus and then to the Sahara. Before the end of the summer of 1148, the area was pacified and 'Abd al-Mu'min travelled to Tinmal to visit the Mahdi's grave. In 1149–50, he gave the shaykhs of the Almohad tribes a list with those to be eliminated for having joined al-Massi's rebellion. In this purge *(i'tiraf)*, more than 32,000 people are said to have been killed.

THE EXPANSION EASTWARDS, THE REBELLION OF IBN TUMART'S BROTHERS AND THE FIGHT AGAINST ARABS AND NORMANS

'Abd al-Mu'min now decided to direct his military efforts towards Ifriqiya, while Almohad troops began intervening in Andalusi matters. In 1150, he had started to build the *ribat al-fath* – now the city of Rabat – on the Atlantic coast, perhaps in order to rival the ribat of Massa. Located on the river Bu Ragrag on the opposite bank to Salé, it was also called al-Mahdiyya, and became the gathering place for the army before caliphal expeditions. 'Abd al-Mu'min knew the importance of controlling the sea for the conquest of both al-Andalus and Ifriqiya, and moreover the site was near the rich agricultural plains of the Gharb and the Tamasna that ensured provisions for the army – underground channels were built to bring water to the new citadel and to irrigate the nearby farmlands.

While in Marrakesh in 1151, 'Abd al-Mu'min decided to name his own sons as governors, thereby diminishing the power of the tribal leaders and Ibn Tumart's family, although some sources date this decision to a later moment. The earlier date would explain why

Ibn Tumart's relatives started to show disaffection around this time, while if the later date is correct it would have been the other way around, with the caliph's decision motivated by the rebelliousness of Ibn Tumart's relatives.

At the end of 1152, an expedition was launched against both the Zirid kingdom of the Banu Hammad who had helped the Almoravids, and the Arab tribes that were pillaging the central and eastern Maghrib. It was also feared that the Arab tribes might forge an alliance with the Normans, although the evidence examined by Tawfiq al-Tibi seems to indicate that these tribes were not inclined to make alliances with Christians against fellow Muslims. The Norman occupation of Ifriqiya had started in 1123, spreading to Tripoli and al-Mahdiyya in 1148. The powerful Almohad army led by the caliph himself took Algiers, where the Zirid ruler of al-Mahdiyya, al-Hasan ibn 'Ali, resided, having fled from Ifriqiya. He joined 'Abd al-Mu'min in his march eastwards. The military commander of Bougie surrendered the town in agreement with the scholars and merchants who had previously contacted the Almohads. The Qal'at Bani Hammad was also taken, and the Arabs who controlled the region were defeated. 'Abd al-Mu'min soon directed his army against Constantine, where the Hammadid king Yahya ibn al-'Aziz had taken refuge. The caliph sent a letter to its inhabitants inviting them to follow the example of Bougie and surrender – which they subsequently did – as well as promising to eliminate all illegal taxes. 'Abd al-Mu'min granted the defeated Hammadid king an estate near Salé, where he died in 1163.

An army led by Yaslasan ibn al-Mu'izz al-Hargi and 'Abd Allah ibn Wanudin al-Hintati fought the Arab tribes that had had the Hammadid kingdom under their 'protectorate' and were greatly annoyed by the Almohad intervention in the area, since it cut off their main source of revenue. Yaslasan and Ibn Wanudin quarrelled, and Yaslasan left to join his relatives, Ibn Tumart's brothers. The Arabs defeated Ibn Wanudin and killed him. 'Abd al-Mu'min confronted them and, by then familiar with the Arab way of fighting in successive attacks (*karr wa-farr*), managed to defeat them. Around this time, a man called Abu Qasaba rebelled near Bougie. 'Abd al-Mu'min participated in the fight against him, personally taking up his spear, which he had not used since the time of the battle of al-Buhayra.

'Abd al-Mu'min then initiated his return to Marrakesh. After his departure, the Yemeni and Hilali Arabs concentrated in the region of Constantine to fight the Almohads who had been left behind to keep them under control. A battle took place in Sétif in May 1153 and the Arabs were defeated. From Tlemcen, 'Abd al-Mu'min sent a letter to Marrakesh with news of the Almohad victory. The caliph brought the Arab chiefs, as well as their women who had been captured, back with him to the capital. He had now to face, on the one hand, the rebellious behaviour of Ibn Tumart's brothers and, on the other, the rebellion of the Gazula, the Lamta and the Banu Igaz in the Sus, in alliance with Ibn al-Sahrawiyya. Abu Hafs 'Umar Inti was put in charge, and he succeeded in 1155 in pacifying the Sus. Ibn al-Sahrawiyya – whose sister was married to Abu Ja'far ibn 'Atiyya, vizier to the caliph – was pardoned by 'Abd al-Mu'min.

Around 1154, 'Abd al-Mu'min named his eldest son Abu 'Abd Allah Muhammad as his heir. Ibn Tumart's brothers – known as the Banu Amgar – had been imprisoned in Fez for their misbehaviour. The nomination of the caliph's son as successor to the Almohad caliphate signalled beyond a doubt that the Banu Amgar would be left out of the power structure their brother had set in motion. They managed to flee Fez for Marrakesh, where they were acclaimed by their followers and killed the governor. However, the muezzin alerted the inhabitants of Marrakesh, who sided with the garrison and confronted the rebels. In the end they were killed, and their corpses hanged at Bab al-Shari'a. Al-Jayyani, the governor of Fez, had in the meantime notified 'Abd al-Mu'min of the brothers' escape, and the caliph sent his secretary Abu Ja'far ibn 'Atiyya to Marrakesh to stop them. When he arrived, their rebellion had already been quashed. He prepared a list with the names of the brothers' supporters, as the letters they had exchanged had been found, revealing their identities. The caliph returned to Marrakesh and had some 300 people detained; he distributed weapons among the inhabitants of Marrakesh, ordered them to form two lines from the gate of the palace to the prison, and had them kill the detainees as they exited the prison.

In 1155–6, 'Abd al-Mu'min travelled to Salé to inspect the construction of Rabat and then returned to Marrakesh. In 1157, the caliph left the capital and travelled through the plains to the north of the High Atlas, then entered the Sus valley and the Anti-Atlas, where he visited Igiliz, before returning via Tinmal. The aim of this trip was to strengthen the allegiance of the original Almohad tribes, and to ensure the submission of the Gazula. On his way back to Marrakesh, the caliph executed Abu Ja'far ibn 'Atiyya, an incident explored in Chapter 7.

A delegation from Zawila, a suburb of al-Mahdiyya, had in the meantime arrived to ask for help against the Normans who had taken it in 1148. 'Abd al-Mu'min left Marrakesh on 26 October 1158, after naming Abu Hafs 'Umar Inti as his delegate in his absence. From Salé, the army moved to Tlemcen, whose governor, the sayyid Abu Hafs, joined the caliph, as did the sayyid 'Abd Allah, governor of Bougie, later on. The Zirid ruler al-Hasan ibn 'Ali also accompanied the caliph on the expedition. The army arrived at Tunis, ruled by the Banu Khurasan, on 13 July 1159. It fell without resistance and, although *aman* was granted to the people, their properties were confiscated. 'Abd al-Mu'min then moved to attack al-Mahdiyya, appointing his relative and new vizier 'Abd al-Salam al-Kumi as governor of Tunis.

Al-Mahdiyya's location made it difficult to take, as the caliph realized when he saw it from a ship. The siege lasted almost six months and the Christians were attacked by land and sea. When the Almohad navy asked permission to attack, 'Abd al-Mu'min knelt to ask for God's help. The Almohad admiral Ibn Maymun – who had formerly served the Almoravids – managed to capture eight Christian ships, while the rest retreated. 'Abd al-Mu'min then prostrated himself to thank God and distributed 12,000 Mu'minid dinars among the crew. At the end of January 1160, the Normans asked for an *aman* for the inhabitants of al-Mahdiyya and their properties, and for permission to leave, as they had run out of provisions. 'Abd al-Mu'min invited them to convert to Islam, but although they refused, he still allowed them to return to Sicily out of fear that if they were executed, King William I might retaliate by massacring the Muslims of Sicily. When they learned of the fall of al-Mahdiyya, the people of Norman-occupied Tripoli and Sfax rose up, pledging their obedience to 'Abd al-Mu'min.

The conquest of heavily fortified Gafsa – also in the hands of the Normans – proved especially difficult. The Arab tribes who controlled most of the territory of Ifriqiya, either directly or indirectly through Berber allies, had also submitted to 'Abd al-Mu'min. However, after 'Abd al-Mu'min left with his army and reached Algiers, he was informed that the Arabs had rebelled. He sent part of his troops to fight them and they were defeated near the mountain of al-Qarn, to the east of Qayrawan, in April 1161. The historicity of this battle has been placed in doubt by Victoria Aguilar, however, as it seems too convenient a counterpart to the great Arab victory of Haydaran in 1052 against the Zirids.

After this victory, 'Abd al-Mu'min took the decision to employ the defeated Arabs in the fight in al-Andalus and began deporting them to the far Maghrib. Returning to Marrakesh, he stopped in Bougie and, passing through a market, remembered that, long ago, he had been there with the Mahdi; not having eaten for several days, he had been forced to sell his inkwell in order to buy some bread. Later, between Batha and Tlemcen, he camped in a place where he had once had to spend the night out in the rain on an empty stomach. Finally, in Tlemcen, he punished his relative 'Abd al-Salam, the vizier, after discovering that he had embezzled booty, among other misdemeanours.

THE CONQUEST OF AL-ANDALUS AND 'ABD AL-MU'MIN'S DEATH

The Almohad conquests between 1141 and 1147 in western Algeria and central and northern Morocco had been greatly helped by the Almoravid military engagement in the Iberian Peninsula. Almoravid defeats at the hands of the Iberian Christians led to unrest and disaffection among the local population. Andalusi judges, as representatives of the urban elites, seized power in cities such as Córdoba, Jaén, Málaga, Murcia and Valencia. Local soldiers trained in the frontier areas, such as Sayf al-dawla ibn Hud, also made bids for power. Likewise, in 1144 the Batini mystic Ibn Qasi rebelled in the Algarve (southern Portugal) at the head of his novices and took control of the area. Ibn Barrajan and Ibn al-‘Arif, two other prominent Andalusi Sufis whose popularity was a matter of concern for the Almoravids, had been summoned to Marrakesh in 1141 and died under suspicious circumstances.

In their fight against the Almoravids, some Andalusis looked to the Almohads. While ‘Abd al-Mu’min was besieging Tlemcen in 1145, Ibn Qasi sent an ambassador offering his submission. The same year, the Almoravid admiral Ibn Maymun delivered the Friday sermon in ‘Abd al-Mu’min’s name at the mosque of Cádiz. During the siege of Marrakesh, the lord of Jerez, Abu l-Ghamr ibn ‘Azzun, and the judge of Córdoba, Ibn Hamdin, among other Andalusi rebels against the Almoravids, sent delegates to ‘Abd al-Mu’min. Ibn Qasi himself crossed the Strait in 1147 to offer his obedience to the caliph, and invited him to send an army to al-Andalus. Ibn Qasi had, like Ibn Tumart, claimed to be the Mahdi: when ‘Abd al-Mu’min reminded him of this claim, Ibn Qasi was quick to retort that everybody knew that there two dawns (*fajr*), one authentic, the other false, and that his Mahdism was of the second type.

‘Abd al-Mu’min sent an army back with Ibn Qasi led by Barraz ibn Muhammad al-Masufi, which arrived in al-Andalus in the summer of 1147. Having occupied Tarifa and Algeciras, they headed towards the Algarve, where Jerez and Niebla submitted; Mértola was taken and given to Ibn Qasi together with Silves, before they moved on to Beja and Badajoz. The next year, Barraz took Seville, and Córdoba was conquered two years later. Almería, an active port town that controlled vital trade routes, fell instead into Christian hands, conquered with the help of the Genoese, and the Almohads only managed to recover it ten years later, in 1157. Lisbon was taken by the king of Portugal with help from Crusaders travelling by sea to Jerusalem. In 1148, the Ebro valley was conquered by the king of Aragon, the same year in which the Normans conquered al-Mahdiyya and Damascus was under siege by the Crusaders.

Almohad control in south-western al-Andalus was soon shaken by revolts in Niebla, Seville and Badajoz. Ibn Qasi rebelled in Silves, al-Bitruji in Niebla and Ibn Maymun in Cádiz. Only Ibn ‘Azzun remained loyal to the Almohads in Jerez and Ronda – once the Almohads regained control, they refrained from confiscating property in this area, and the

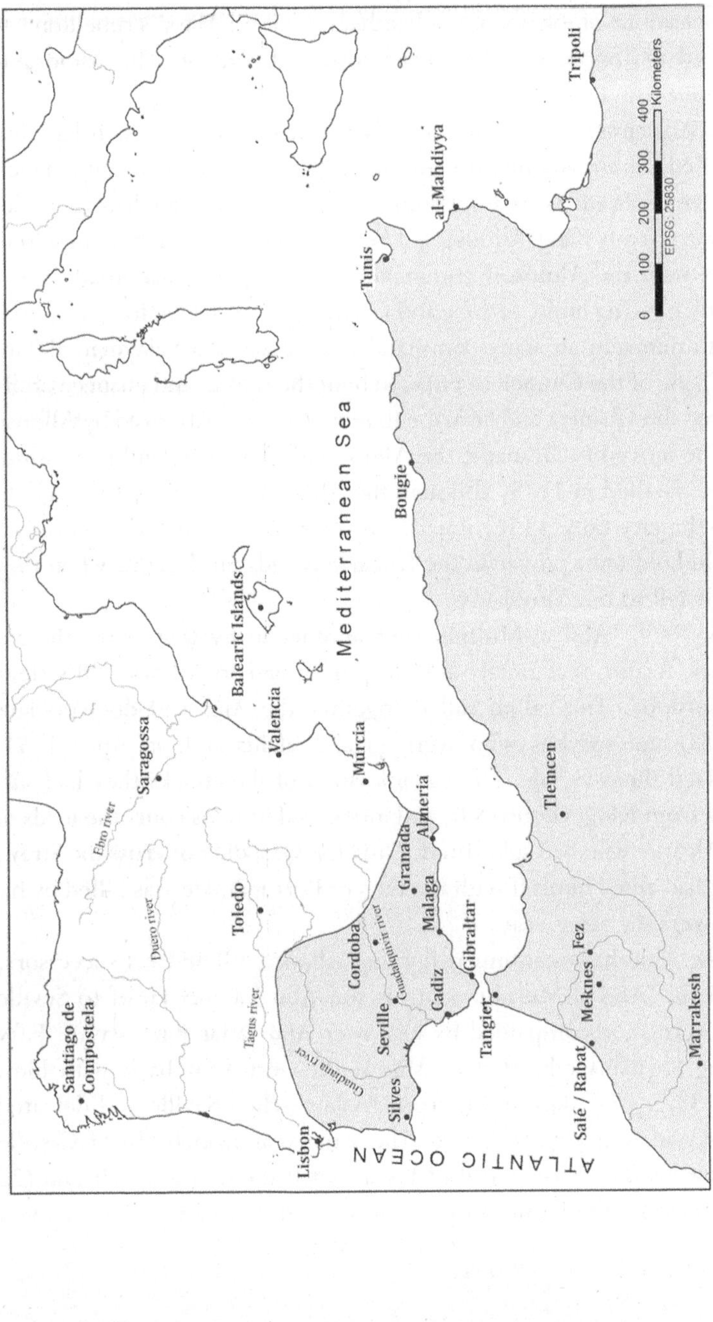

Map 4 *The Almohad empire at the time of ‘Abd al-Mu’min (© CCHS-CSIC).*

Banu 'Azzun were given priority among the Andalusi delegates to the Almohad court. The underlying disaffection had been caused by the misbehaviour of Ibn Tumart's brothers, while al-Massi's rebellion had offered the opportunity to shake Almohad control. The Almoravid Ibn Ghaniya al-Masufi still controlled some parts of al-Andalus and took Algeciras, sending Ibn al-Sahrawiyya to Ceuta, which had also rebelled. As already mentioned, Ibn Tumart's brothers eventually left the Peninsula and were imprisoned in Fez in 1153. Ibn Ghaniya, under pressure from King Alfonso VII (r. 1126–1157), reached an agreement with the Almohad commander Barraz ibn Muhammad (also a Masufi), giving him Córdoba and Carmona in exchange for Jaén. 'Abd al-Mu'min sent an army commanded by Yusuf ibn Sulayman al-Tinmali, one of the Council of Fifty, to fight the rebels, and unsuccessfully invited Ibn Ghaniya and his tribe to join *al-tawhid*. Attacked by Alfonso VII, he moved to Granada, the Almoravids' last mainland possession, where he died in 1149, although the Almohads would not manage to take the city until 1156. Ibn Ghaniya's relatives, the Banu Ghaniya, would hold onto power in the Balearic Islands until 1202, when they finally fell to the Almohads.

In 1149, 'Abd al-Mu'min sent another army that, with the aid of Ibn 'Azzun, was finally able to put an end to Alfonso VII's siege of Córdoba. The caliph called together the Almohad doctrinarians (*talaba*) and shaykhs who were in al-Andalus and, in April 1151, received them in Salé. He was informed of the attacks they had suffered from King Alfonso VII, and integrated into his court the lords of the Algarve who had submitted. Only Ibn Qasi did not cross the Strait, as he had allied himself with the king of Portugal. He was killed by his followers the same year.

The Almohads continued fighting Alfonso VII and his successors. In 1156, 'Abd al-Mu'min sent his son Abu Ya'qub Yusuf to Seville as governor, accompanied by his vizier Abu Ja'far ibn 'Atiyya. Fifty young Sevillans educated in Marrakesh were sent back with him. In 1158, a Christian militia from Ávila reached Seville and defeated the sayyid Abu Ya'qub Yusuf. The same year, Sancho III of Castille and his brother Fernando II of León signed the treaty of Sahagún (23 May 1158), stipulating into which Muslim territories each of them would expand their domains. Also in 1158, the local military order of Calatrava was founded, and 'Abd al-Mu'min began his campaign to conquer Ifriqiya.

The Almohads in al-Andalus had to confront not only the Christians but also the Muslim ruler of Murcia, Ibn Mardanish and his father-in-law, Ibn Hamushk, who, sometimes in alliance with the Christians, sought to expand towards Jaén – successfully captured in 1159 – and Granada. They also attacked and ravaged the region of Córdoba. In February–March 1160, as Ibn Hamushk was threatening Seville, the sayyid Abu Ya'qub Yusuf asked his father for help. 'Abd al-Mu'min gave instructions to start fortifying Gibraltar in order to make it impregnable. He was now to direct his attention to the western part of his empire, employing the Arabs of Ifriqiya in al-Andalus; through jihad, he claimed, they could redeem their sins.

In November 1160, 'Abd al-Mu'min embarked on his sole trip to al-Andalus, crossing the Strait from Ceuta to Gibraltar, in order to oversee the situation at a moment when Seville and Córdoba were under siege and Granada was insecure. Military intervention was not so much on his mind as were the acknowledgement of his religious and political authority, however. During his two-month stay, he received delegations, poets recited verses exalting him, and the Festival of Sacrifice was celebrated. He confirmed his sons as governors of Seville and Granada, and named Abu Hafs 'Umar Inti governor of Córdoba, before leaving in January 1161.

After returning to Marrakesh, 'Abd al-Mu'min sent an army under the command of the experienced Yusuf ibn Sulayman to take provisions and weapons to Córdoba. It garrisoned in Seville to help against the threat from Carmona, which had been taken by Ibn Hamushk. It then returned to Marrakesh with the two sayyids to organize a major offensive against al-Andalus.

In the meantime, in December 1162, Carmona was reconquered by the Almohads, but Ibn Hamushk took Granada with the help of the Almoravids, the Christians and the Jews of Granada, whom the Almohads had forced to convert. The Almohads resisted in the citadel and Ibn Hamushk requested reinforcements. Ibn Mardanish arrived with Christian mercenaries. The caliph had just left Marrakesh for

Rabat to prepare the expedition against al-Andalus with a huge army that included the Arabs brought from Ifriqiya. Given the urgency of the situation, 'Abd al-Mu'min sent one of his sons with troops who asked the governor of Seville to join them. Together they advanced towards Granada but were defeated en route by Ibn Hamushk. In response, 'Abd al-Mu'min sent more troops, again under the command of Yusuf ibn Sulayman, who launched a surprise attack against Ibn Hamushk and his Christian mercenaries. Ibn Mardanish and Ibn Hamushk were forced to retreat from Granada and those who had helped them were punished, with the Almohads confiscating their properties.

'Abd al-Mu'min then ordered the repopulation of Córdoba, whose population had been reduced to some eighty inhabitants. The rest of the population had fled, while those who stayed behind had begun to farm the land inside the city walls as a remedy for the famine caused by the conflict. The caliph also ordered that Córdoba be restored as the capital of al-Andalus, naming as its governor the Almoravid Barraz al-Masufi. As Pascal Buresi has noted, at this point 'Abd al-Mu'min was intent in bolstering his legitimacy by connecting his caliphate to that of the Cordoban Umayyads, having previously transferred to Marrakesh the copy of the Qur'an of 'Uthman that had allegedly been preserved in the Cordoban mosque. Córdoba, however, would not be the capital for long: shortly after 'Abd al-Mu'min's death, his successor Abu Ya'qub Yusuf, who had been living in Seville for six years, restored its status as capital.

During the autumn and winter of 1162, 'Abd al-Mu'min ordered a powerful fleet to be built, and men were recruited and provisions and weapons were prepared. During this period, the Portuguese took Beja and held it for several months. Before launching the campaign against al-Andalus, 'Abd al-Mu'min decided to embark on an extremely difficult journey, braving the cold and rain, to visit Tinmal. When fording the river Nafis on horseback, the water reached up to his knees. After visiting the Mahdi's grave, he returned to Marrakesh, and on 21 February 1162 moved on to Rabat. 'Abd al-Mu'min stated his intention to simultaneously attack by sea and land all four Christian kingdoms – Portugal, León, Castille and Aragon. However, just as he was departing, he fell sick with the illness that would eventually lead to his death.

Although the sources are not unanimous on the matter, it appears that during this period 'Abd al-Mu'min ordered that the name of his son Muhammad, the heir apparent, should stop being mentioned in the Friday prayer. Instead, he named Abu Ya'qub Yusuf his new heir, instructing him to trust Abu Hafs 'Umar Inti and Yusuf ibn Sulayman, to simply wait for Ibn Mardanish to die rather than waste effort attacking him, and to use the Arabs of Ifriqiya in the Iberian Peninsula.

'Abd al-Mu'min died on Tuesday 14 May 1163. He had reigned for thirty-three years, counting since the Mahdi's death. He was buried at the feet of the Mahdi in Tinmal.

JIHAD, THE ARMY AND THE COLLECTION OF TAXES

Ibn Tumart claimed that those who did not go over to his side and fight with him should be killed together with their families, as his uprising against the Almoravids was for the sake of God. In the letters attributed to him, he insisted that the jihad against the Almoravids was more important than that against the Christians. Thus, Ibn Tumart applied a radical interpretation of the Islamic doctrines on jihad and rebellion, justified because the rulers of the time had departed from the fundamental tenets of Islam. But he went even further, asserting that all the earth's inhabitants were in fact the slaves of his close companions who formed the Council of Ten. This doctrine is mentioned in a number of episodes, implying, on the one hand, that it was meaningful for the early Almohads and, on the other, that it became a source of embarrassment, as there was nothing in Islamic doctrine that could justify it. What this suggests is that the ways in which the early Almohads and their Masmuda audience understood their fight against the Almoravids may not have been exactly in accordance with standard Islamic norms.

At the end of the campaign against Ifriqiya, he told the Arabs that, just as their ancestors had conquered al-Andalus centuries before, the time had come for them to conquer it again. His intended targets were not only the Christians, but also Muslim rulers like Ibn Mardanish who had not yet submitted to *al-tawhid*. The Arabs, however, were not convinced, and some of them fled, discredited by Ibn Sahib al-salat as having performed apostasy (*ridda*), just as the Arabs had done after the Prophet Muhammad's death. Ibn Sahib al-salat referred to the military intervention of the Almohads in Granada as jihad because, even if the war was waged against Andalusi Muslims, they were enemies of the Almohads and, moreover, had allied themselves with the Christians. As shown by Linda Jones, Ibn Sahib al-salat constantly conveyed the idea that the Almohads were helped by God and that their victories were the result of divine agency. Almohad violence, regardless of its intensity and even cruelty, was always legitimate, and that of their opponents, even if it was exactly the same, was regarded as a clear sign of their evil and Satanic character. The caliph 'Abd al-Mu'min was represented as a paradigmatic ruler in his relation to God, always defending truth and defeating error. Ibn al-Qattan claimed that some verses of the Cordoban poet Ibn 'Abd Rabbihi (d. 940) dealing with the Mahdi referenced 'Abd al-Mu'min as 'lord of the conquests and master of the final battles' (*rabb al-futuh wa-sahib al-malahim*), thus endowing him with an eschatological aura.

'Abd al-Mu'min initially took part in the fighting as he had in the battle of al-Buhayra, but afterwards refrained from personal involvement in battle – except during the aforementioned rebellion of Abu Qasaba. The sources do not offer narratives of his personal bravery and military exploits, but undoubtedly Ibn Tumart's bid for power as a Mahdi led to an empire thanks only to 'Abd al-Mu'min's political and military abilities.

The early Almohad hierarchical organization had at its summit the Council of Ten formed by the Mahdi's closest companions (*jama'a*), followed by the Council of Fifty formed by the shaykhs of the tribes (Masmuda and others) that had joined the Almohad cause. Each tribe had two military officers (*mizwar*), one for those who had joined the Almohad cause early on and another for those who had joined it later. Only the Harga had one *mizwar*. The Almohad army was thus initially a tribal army formed mostly by Masmuda. The tribes were periodically submitted to purges to keep their discipline and fitness in check. Precedence in having joined *al-tawhid* established a hierarchical ranking among the Almohads.

The Almoravid army had also been tribal, based on the Sanhaja from the desert and especially on the Lamtuna confederation. The Almoravid army had also included Christian mercenaries (*rum*), one contingent of whom left for Christian Spain once Marrakesh fell, while another went over to the Almohads, who employed them, for example, against al-Massi. Little is said about them afterwards, but they would become a crucial element under the caliph al-Ma'mun (r. 1227–1228) because of his conflict with the Almohad shaykhs. The Almoravid army also included salaried troops (*hasham*) from the Masmuda, Zanata, Gazula and Lamta – these last two were Sanhaja but did not belong to the Lamtuna confederation. Part of these salaried troops joined the Almohads. The Gazula, one of the most powerful tribes of the south-eastern region of the Anti-Atlas, joined *al-tawhid* around 1140–1; their tribal council (*agraw*) was then convened by 'Abd al-Mu'min, who took on the role of deciding whose turn it was to speak at the assembly. As noted by Ghouirgate, traditional Berber institutions with a horizontal character such as the *agraw* were at this time made to evolve towards a more vertical structure, as power became more and more concentrated in the person of 'Abd al-Mu'min and his family. In al-Andalus, individual notables and lineages (such as the Banu 'Azzun) also joined *al-tawhid*, and some even joined the Almohad army, but this was a development that mostly took place after 'Abd al-Mu'min's death, when Almohad control was more firmly established. The Almohad army thus reflected the broad variety of the Almohad empire.

The Almohad army also included other groups such as the black slaves of the Almoravids (*'abid al-makhzan*). J. F. P. Hopkins argues that the drummers (*tabbala*) were connected to the *'abid*, as in his opinion drums should be associated with sub-Saharan Africa. There were also archers probably selected from among the Almohad tribesmen, while the 'raiders' (*ghuzat*) seem to have been recruits to the Almohad cause uninstructed in the creed; in 'Abd al-Mu'min's times, they are mentioned in connection with the fleet. Among the groups that formed part of the army, mention is made of those in charge of minting coinage (*sakkakun*). There were also muezzins who travelled with the army to deliver the call to prayer. Non-tribal elements, such as the people of Aghmat and other city dwellers, formed the *jund*, a term usually employed to refer to regular, professional soldiers who received payment whether they were fighting or not. As Hopkins has noted, this type of full-time troops with no tribal loyalties tended to form the ruler's personal guard.

The tribal components of the army only took up arms when called on for a campaign. Under 'Abd al-Mu'min, his own Kumya tribe was incorporated into the Almohad army, as were the Arabs defeated in the central Maghrib (Sulaym, Hilal, Khult and Sufyan). In 1161 some of them were settled in the regions of al-Hibt and Tamasna, in a relocation campaign that would become more widespread later on. Both the Kumya and the Arabs were useful for counterbalancing the power of the Masmuda tribal shaykhs when necessary.

The chronicle *al-Hulul al-mawshiyya* records how the Almohad army operated. After performing the dawn prayer, a huge dark-coloured circular drum sounded three times; it could be heard from half a day's journey away, and signalled it was time to depart. 'Abd al-Mu'min, surrounded by notables, mounted his horse, preceded by 100 horsemen and by the copy of the Qur'an of 'Uthman brought from Córdoba and transported on a she-camel. He was followed by his sons, the sayyids, presided by the heir apparent. Next came the flags and drums and the high functionaries of the empire, followed by the rest of the army in perfect order. The army was divided into four sections, each of which occupied a fixed position when camping. They also had banners of different colours; at the time of Ibn Tumart, white had been assigned to 'Abd al-Mu'min, and this was the colour that continued to be associated with him and his successors, which was especially apt as they claimed the legacy of the Andalusi Umayyads. The daily march lasted until lunchtime, after which the army rested until the following day. The army brought along artisans capable of crafting or mending any item they might possibly need.

The Zirid prince Ibn Shaddad, who took part in the expedition against Ifriqiya, noted that the soldiers said the five daily prayers and that they respected the harvests of the territories they passed through. The vanguard was formed by 12,000 men who stayed two days in advance of the others in order to dig wells to ensure the provision of water. Almohad armies were famous for the huge numbers they mobilized, which made them quite expensive to maintain. They were also slow: in 1158, it took six months for the army to move from Salé to Tunis, a distance that on horseback would normally take just seventy days. Provisions such as grain had to be stored in advance in underground pits. The vast size of the Almohad empire made it difficult to attend every possible front. For all its military might, many areas that formed part of the Almohad empire, such as southern Algeria, must have retained a high degree of autonomy, with the Almohads resorting to local forces to secure a certain degree of control.

The sources stress the high degree of discipline in 'Abd al-Mu'min's army. Soldiers were ordered not to divulge the real destination of the expeditions; once, when a black slave mentioned out loud what they were planning to do once they reached Bougie, he was executed. Al-Yasa' ibn Hazm (d. 1179) described the technique that secured the Almohads' victory in the battle of Mindas, but, as in other cases, his trustworthiness is to be doubted. In his account, the Almohad troops formed a square with the infantry on each side armed with long spears and shields; behind them was a second row of soldiers armed with javelins; behind this row were the slingers; in the fourth row, the archers; and in the centre of the square the cavalry waited. When attacked, they fought with the spears, stones and arrows. When the attackers backed away, the Almohad cavalry made its appearance and, if the enemy returned to the offensive, they fell back into the well-protected centre of the square.

The Almoravid admiral, Ibn Maymun, had defected to the Almohads in 1146, bringing with him not only the entire fleet under his command, but also his valuable expertise. The caliph was in fact as interested in developing the navy as the Fatimids and the Zirids had been: under their rule, the maritime towns of Bougie, Tunis, Mahdiyya, Sousse and Tripoli had flourished. Having been born in Hammadid territory, 'Abd al-Mu'min must have been aware of this, and in his military expeditions the navy played an important role. He knew how to swim, and swimming was one of the skills that all *talaba* had to learn. Interest in maritime matters was passed on to 'Abd al-Mu'min's successors as vital for the economic and military development of the empire, and they favoured trade with both Muslim and Christian polities.

The Christian conquest of Almería in 1147 had highlighted the strategic importance of controlling Ceuta. In 1156, 'Abd al-Mu'min organized the area around the Strait of Gibraltar into a single province, an administrative and military decision that helped regain the port of Almería in 1157. The constructions in Gibraltar made it possible to reinforce the caliph's control over the area, and were instrumental in ensuring the conquest of the Andalusi territories that continued to hold out against the Almohads, such as the Levant (Sharq al-Andalus), which finally submitted in 1172. Rabat was under the direct control of the caliph and an arsenal was built at the mouth of the Sebou river. 'Abd al-Mu'min thus made it clear that he intended to control both land and sea, including not only the Mediterranean but also the Atlantic coast, with the ports of Safi and Azemmour.

The Almoravids had introduced the custom of rewarding military and other types of service with grants of land (*iqta'at*) and the Almohads followed suit. The Almohad *iqta'*, on which the sources offer unclear information, has been studied by 'Izz al-din 'Umar Musa, Yassir Benhima and Amar Baadj, among others. Ibn Tumart had assigned some of the conquered lands to the Almohad tribes as 'rewards' (*ja'iza*, plural *jawa'iz*), equivalent to *iqta' tamlik*, that is, as land held privately by the tribe on the condition that the grantee paid certain taxes to the state. In the early period, the lands conquered from Muslim rulers were treated in the same way that non-Muslim lands had been treated during the Islamic conquests: properties and possessions were considered booty with one-fifth going to the state and the rest divided up among the Almohad conquerors. In 1147–8, many Muslims in conquered territories who had suffered such treatment rose up in protest, leading 'Abd al-Mu'min to put an end to the practice, and to embrace all those who accepted Almohad rule. The lands taken from the Muslims were no longer treated as spoils of war to be confiscated by the victors.

Iqta'at were granted not only as a reward to powerful tribal chiefs, but also as compensation to appease defeated rebels and members of former ruling dynasties. They were also granted to bureaucrats and even to poets. Musa believes that these *iqta'at* were of the usufruct type, that is, revenue from a piece of land was apportioned in place of a salary. According to Benhima, who agrees with Musa, the system was highly centralized and under the control of the state: its agents managed the *iqta'* lands, collected the revenues and paid the grantees out of the revenue; the grantee did not play a direct role in the exploitation of the *iqta'*. The transfer of these grants from one individual to another was closely controlled by the state. Benhima and Baaj hold different positions regarding whether the stipends paid to the Almohad soldiers complemented the regular income they received from estates (*siham*) granted to them, or the other way around. They also differ as to whether the soldiers were directly involved in farming these estates.

Initially, the Almohads had subsisted off confiscations and the booty taken from the Almoravids and other enemies. A number of reports paint a very dark picture of the destruction and famine that ensued. In his history of Meknes, Ibn Ghazi explains that many of its inhabitants lost ownership of their agricultural properties, but were forced to continue working them subject to abusive taxation conducted by unscrupulous intermediaries (*qashshashun*) between them and the state (*makhzan*). Many fled, simply abandoning their fields. Eventually, reforms were made that improved the situation. In the *Risalat al-fusul*, the caliph exhorted the Almohads to give the obligatory alms (*zakat*) and this seems to signal the moment when they were subject to taxation. When returning from the conquest of Ifriqiya, 'Abd al-Mu'min had complained of financial problems and it was then that a land census of his empire was undertaken for *kharaj* (land tax) purposes. He ordered

> a survey (*taksir*) of the lands of Ifriqiya and the Maghrib, and it was surveyed from Ifriqiya and Barqa...to the country of Nul in Farthest Sus, by parasangs and miles, in length and breadth. He omitted from the survey a third corresponding with mountains, scrub, rivers, salt-pans, roads, and ravines, and apportioned (*qassata*) over the rest the *kharaj* and

> obliged every tribe to pay its proportion...in corn and coin... He was the first in the Maghrib to do this.
>
> (Translation by J. F. P. Hopkins, 1958)

The obscurity and difficulties posed by this passage found in Ibn Abi Zar''s chronicle have been duly analyzed by Hopkins. He concludes that this *kharaj* was a tax on productive land that disregarded the legal norms, as it implied that all Muslims who were not Almohads were unbelievers and that the Almohads were therefore entitled to take their properties.

4

BALANCING POWER TO ACHIEVE DYNASTIC RULE: THE ALMOHAD HIERARCHIES

IBN TUMART'S FAMILY AND INNER CIRCLE: THE *AHL AL-DAR* AND THE COUNCIL OF TEN

The nature of the sources at our disposal makes it difficult to reconstruct the social and religious background into which Ibn Tumart was born. Was Ibn Tumart a self-made leader or was he helped by his family status? Two main views have been proposed regarding this issue, both of which rely heavily on Ibn Tumart's name. His onomastic chain is given as Muhammad ibn Tumart ibn Ugallid ibn Waburkan, although he must have also had a Berber first name, perhaps Asafu. According to the trend that transformed Ibn Tumart into an Arab, his father's real name would have been 'Abd Allah in Arabic (the Mahdi's name had to be that of the Prophet Muhammad, whose father was called 'Abd Allah), Tumart being a Berber term meaning 'joy'. Ibn Tumart's paternal uncle was Waburkan ibn Ugallid and his paternal aunt was Hawwa' bint Ugallid. Waburkan also shows up in connection with Ibn Tumart's mother, Umm al-Husayn bint Waburkan al-Masakkali.

Ibn Tumart referred to his father respectfully as *amgar*, i.e. as a tribal elder. But according to Ghouirgate, the humble origins of Ibn Tumart's father are revealed in an anecdote in the *Kitab al-ansab* in which the Mahdi asked his tribesmen, who had gathered around him, to make way for his father, which would indicate that he was not receiving the automatic respect usually accorded to a person of high standing. According to Ghouirgate, Ibn Tumart's family may have even descended from enslaved sub-Saharan Africans, as Waburkan (he who has *baraka*) was a name often given to slaves; the Berber names Ugallid (king) or Umsal (blacksmith) that appear in the onomastic chains attributed to Ibn Tumart would not have been original but rather produced in order to enhance his status. By contrast, van Staëvel takes these names at face value, and with them the possibility that Ibn Tumart belonged to a family that enjoyed pre-eminent social standing. He proposes that the tribal milieu in which Ibn Tumart was born was already familiar with what Max Weber termed 'traditional domination', that is, power founded on personal legitimacy inscribed in a family tradition and exerted by means of servants and dependants.

Members of Ibn Tumart's family may have been the founders of the Ribat of the Harga. For van Staëvel, when Ibn Tumart's father is referred to as *amgar*, this is a reference to a tribal chief, someone with a leading position. The name of Ibn Tumart's grandfather, Ugallid, refers to the Berber term *agellid*, equivalent to a powerful king. For van Staëvel, this evokes a traditional form of domination, a lineage that produced in three generations a 'king' (*agellid*, Ibn Tumart's grandfather), a tribal chief (*amgar*, Ibn Tumart's father), and finally an *imam mahdi*, Ibn Tumart himself. If this *nasab* reflects a historical situation, in the second generation there was a loss of power that could be explained by the fact that the function of the *agellid* was not hereditary, and also by the establishment of the Almoravid empire in the region, which would have affected the status of locally rooted 'big men'. In any case, this would imply that Ibn Tumart's trajectory was not exclusively dependent on his personal charisma, but also on a family legacy of leadership. Moreover, if the Ribat of the Harga preceded Ibn Tumart, the nature of his grandfather's power may already have been shaped by a religious message. If Ibn Tumart belonged to a sacred lineage, his case would thus be similar to that of the Berber *igurramen* (saints), as proposed by Madeleine Fletcher.

Very little is known about Ibn Tumart's father, and even less about his mother, who was from a place called Ansa. Ibn Tumart's father did not move to Tinmal, as there are reports that when news of his death reached the Mahdi at Tinmal, he cried. Ibn Tumart's uterine sister Zaynab lived with Ibn Tumart and was present when he died. Ibn Tumart never married, and he is not known to have had any offspring. His relatives, referred to as Ayt Amgar or Banu Amgar, appear in the historical record in relation to the troubles they caused 'Abd al-Mu'min.

Ibn Tumart's three brothers were Abu Musa 'Isa, Abu Muhammad 'Abd al-'Aziz and Abu l-'Abbas Ahmad; their original Berber names are unknown. Ahmad was blind and did not take part in political activities. What we are told about the other two brothers is never positive. They took part in the conquest of al-Andalus in 1147 and resided with their large household in Seville. Their conduct is characterized as being so inappropriate and unjust that they are presented as the main cause for the Andalusi revolt that threatened Almohad control over Gharb al-Andalus.

Yaslasan ibn al-Mu'izz al-Hargi was another relative of Ibn Tumart, perhaps a son of his sister. In 1151, 'Abd al-Mu'min sent him with 'Abd Allah ibn Wanudin al-Hintati – the husband of one of the caliph's daughters – to fight the Arabs in the Sétif region, but the Almohads were defeated and Ibn Wanudin taken captive, apparently because Yaslasan betrayed him after having insulted his wife. Yaslasan then took refuge in Seville with his relatives, Ibn Tumart's brothers, but was eventually captured and executed in Ceuta. Later, in 1154, as mentioned in the previous chapter, Ibn Tumart's brothers took Marrakesh by surprise, but were defeated and killed. 'Abd al-Mu'min took care to explain in one of his letters that he had always treated them well; their fate was thus the consequence of their own wrongdoing. We will never be able to hear their side of the story.

Both Zaynab and Yaslasan were members of the 'people of the house' (*ahl al-dar*). Other members were individuals who became attached to Ibn Tumart as his personal servants. The *Kitab al-ansab* lists twenty names, among them 'Abd al-Wahid ibn 'Umar al-Sharqi. Abu Muhammad Wasnar was a black tanner from Aghmat; he was pious and extremely discreet, and for this reason Ibn Tumart put him in charge of his personal care, and of controlling who was admitted to his presence. During the three years in which Ibn Tumart's death was kept secret, he acted as the transmitter of the Mahdi's alleged orders. He later became the guardian of Ibn Tumart's grave and that of 'Abd al-Mu'min, until he died very old and poor. The letter sent in 1153 from Tlemcen in which 'Abd al-Mu'min announced the victory over the Arabs in Sétif was addressed to him and to the people of Marrakesh, which means that he had been left behind as the caliph's delegate, a position that indicates how much trust 'Abd al-Mu'min had in him.

Another member of the *ahl al-dar* was Ibrahim ibn Jami', originally from Toledo. He grew up near Cádiz and from there moved to the Maghrib, where he joined Ibn Tumart. Ibrahim ibn Jami' and his descendants, despite not belonging to any of the Masmuda tribes and therefore lacking noble status, rose to prominence in the administration and became very wealthy – in the courtyard of the Banu Jami''s house in Marrakesh, 500 women were able to perform a war game in which they mounted wooden horses. Ibrahim ibn Jami''s sons grew up with the Mu'minid princes and held important positions for a long time. Here, as in the case of Abu Muhammad Wasnar, the ties of loyalty established with Ibn Tumart were transferred to 'Abd al-Mu'min, to the advantage of a man who, like them, lacked any Masmuda connection. Upon reaching his homeland in 1142–3, 'Abd al-Mu'min attracted new supporters such as the Banu Wamannu, one of whom, Abu Warzig al-Zanati, also became part of the *ahl al-dar*. By then this expression referred to those who served the caliph. Little more is said about the *ahl al-dar* from this point onwards.

Ibn Tumart's companions who formed the Council of Ten (*al-jama'a*) were closely involved in the Mahdi's religious and political activities, as we have seen in the case of 'Abd al-Mu'min. Ibn Tumart declared that everybody in this world were the slaves of these men – unconditional followers described as 'the salt of the earth' – and their descendants. Nothing similar was attributed to *al-'ashara al-mubashshara*, the Ten to whom the Arab Prophet Muhammad promised Paradise and the counterpart of the Almohad Council of Ten. Ibn

Tumart had met his Ten during his travels through North Africa and none of them belonged to his Harga tribe, although some came from tribes that were also part of the Masmuda tribal confederation. The Mahdi attached some of them, such as 'Abd al-Mu'min and al-Bashir al-Wansharisi, to the Harga via links of 'brotherhood'. Some of these early companions died before Ibn Tumart at the battle of al-Buhayra, including al-Bashir al-Wansharisi, who seems to have been the real 'second-in-command': he was not only an early companion, but one with special powers, as already mentioned. Had he survived the battle of al-Buhayra, he would have been a clear rival for Ibn Tumart's succession.

Abu 'Imran Musa ibn Tamara al-Gadmiwi, who headed the Council as *amin* or *mizwar*, and Abu Yahya (or Abu Bakr) ibn Igit al-Hintati were both Masmuda. They also died at the battle of al-Buhayra, as did Abu l-Rabi' Sulayman ibn Makhluf al-Hadri, from Aghmat, who acted as Ibn Tumart's secretary, undoubtedly because he was an Arabic speaker. Among the rest, two more were also Masmuda. Abu Ibrahim Isma'il Igig ibn Isallali al-Hazraji, who had protected Ibn Tumart while he was travelling through the Atlas Mountains towards Igiliz, took part in military expeditions and acted as judge in Tinmal. He offered to substitute 'Abd al-Mu'min in his bed when an attack against the caliph was expected on the part of Ibn Tumart's brothers, and died as a result, a tale that may in fact have been a way of covering up 'Abd al-Mu'min's murder of a potential rival. His descendants intermarried with the Mu'minids. Abu 'Abd Allah Muhammad ibn Sulayman, who came from the same village as Ibn Tumart's mother, was in charge of leading the prayer.

Two other members of the Council were not Masmuda; one of them, Abu Hafs 'Umar ibn 'Ali Asnag, was Sanhaja. He presided over the proclamation of 'Abd al-Mu'min as the Mahdi's successor – a succession for which he had also been proposed, since he was a foreigner like 'Abd al-Mu'min. While fighting in the Seven-Year Campaign he fell ill, but refused to take shelter in a tent, declaring that he would not sit in the shade while the rest of the Almohads remained under the sun. After having exhorted his fellow men to obey 'Abd al-Mu'min, he died in 1142–3. One of his sons also played an important role in

Almohad history. As for 'Abd Allah ibn Ya'la Ibn Malwiya, he fought in the battle of al-Buhayra and rebelled in 1133, as he did not agree with 'Abd al-Mu'min's succession: curiously, he was like him a Zanata. He was killed by the Gadmiwa.

Among those who survived Ibn Tumart's death, Abu Hafs 'Umar ibn Yahya Inti (al-Hintati) is usually considered the second most important figure during and after 'Abd al-Mu'min's reign. Abu Hafs 'Umar Inti was a member of the Hintata, a Masmuda tribe established on the northern side of the High Atlas Mountains, where they controlled the Tizi n'Test pass and thus the passage between the Sus and the Hawz of Marrakesh. Abu Hafs 'Umar Inti's Berber name was Faskat ibn Umzal. Ibn Tumart met him and his father when moving from Aghmat to Igiliz. The year was 1121; Faskat must have been in his twenties. He led the Hintata in the fourth expedition organized by the Mahdi, who gave him his leather shield, and later he was injured in the battle of al-Buhayra. Ibn Khaldun tends to highlight his relevance, for example stating that it was Abu Hafs 'Umar Inti who announced the Mahdi's death and proclaimed 'Abd al-Mu'min as his successor. This should be viewed in connection to the fact that the historian worked for the post-Almohad Hafsid dynasty in Ifriqiya. The Hafsids were Abu Hafs 'Umar Inti's descendants and drew their legitimacy from their ancestor's association with Ibn Tumart, and thus had a vested interest in representing him as especially close to the Mahdi – a concern that an earlier historian, al-Baydhaq, who died before the Hafsid dynasty was established, did not have, which explains why he paid much less attention to Abu Hafs 'Umar Inti. He was one of the shaykhs commanding the troops with whom 'Abd al-Mu'min carried out the conquest of the far Maghrib and eastern Algeria, and afterwards of Marrakesh. An episode dated to 1142–3, to be dealt with in greater depth below, indicates the special authority that he had as a member of the Council of Ten.

Abu Hafs 'Umar Inti's role increased in relevance when rebellions erupted that threatened the Almohads' very survival, when for example he was made commander of the army sent to combat al-Massi. Likewise, when 'Abd al-Mu'min left for the campaign in Ifriqiya, he named Abu Hafs 'Umar Inti as his delegate. Abu

Hafs 'Umar Inti's most decisive intervention was to support 'Abd al-Mu'min when he named his son Muhammad as his successor around 1154, thereby moving the Almohad polity towards dynastic rule. After Muhammad fell in disgrace, he eventually supported Abu Ya'qub Yusuf as caliph and served him loyally in various capacities until his death in 1176 at the age of seventy, fifty-seven years after first meeting Ibn Tumart.

Abu Hafs 'Umar Inti does not seem to have ever posed a real threat to 'Abd al-Mu'min. First of all, his prestige among the Almohads could never match that of the older 'Abd al-Mu'min, who was one of Ibn Tumart's earliest companions. Moreover, the fact that Abu Hafs 'Umar Inti had a Masmuda tribe behind him may not have been an asset, as the other tribes in the confederation would have resented his ascension. Also, it is not clear that he was Arabized, as 'Abd al-Mu'min was – a crucial asset for running an empire that had transcended its original Berber roots. Abu Hafs 'Umar Inti seems to have thought that his fortune and that of his family was dependant on 'Abd al-Mu'min, and he was right: his direct descendants and other relatives occupied important positions in the imperial administration, and, as mentioned, one of his grandsons, Abu Zakariyya' Yahya, profited from the fact that the Almohad caliph al-Ma'mun had abandoned the Almohad doctrine and attacked the Almohad shaykhs, in order to proclaim himself independent as defender of the purity of the Almohad tradition. The founder of the Hafsid dynasty ruled from 1228 to 1249, and Hafsid rule lasted in Ifriqiya until 1526.

The members of the *ahl al-dar* and the Council of Ten were decisive in the success of the Almohad cause. Their belief in the Mahdi and their willingness to follow and serve him gave legitimacy to his religious and political authority, and helped broadcast it to a wider audience. Those who were not Masmuda seem to have been the ones who were considered for the Mahdi's succession, but among them 'Abd al-Mu'min stood out for his early link with Ibn Tumart and his knowledge of Arabic. The other Zanata on the Council, Ibn Malwiya, was the only one who publicly opposed 'Abd al-Mu'min's succession, a stance that would cost him his life.

THE ALMOHAD TRIBES, THE COUNCIL OF FIFTY AND THE SHAYKHS

Ibn Tumart and his followers established contact with the tribal milieu of the Atlas Mountains during their journey from Aghmat to Igiliz. The *Kitab al-ansab* gives detailed lists of the tribes that adhered to the Almohad cause, together with those that al-Bashir al-Wansharisi linked to them by bonds of fraternity. There are other less complete lists, all of which include the Harga, Hintata, Gadmiwa and Ganfisa. Once settled in Igiliz, such contact was intensified by sending missionaries to the Hazmira and the Hintata, and through the impact of the military activities conducted against the Almoravids, especially after the move to Tinmal, when still more tribes joined. As mentioned, it is difficult to recover what exactly appealed to the tribesmen's imagination or needs that made them adhere to the Almohad movement: was it Ibn Tumart's charisma? The religious message of the uncompromising *tawhid*? The fact that the Almohad victories were seen as proof of the Truth of the Mahdi's teachings? The allure of booty? Resentment against Almoravid dominance? Different reasons must have existed according to each tribe and time.

Although we cannot reconstruct the variety of ways in which the reception of Ibn Tumart's message unfolded, what is clear is that this reception must not be conceptualized as passive. The Sus area had already experienced some degree of Islamization under the influence of diverse Islamic religious and political messages, including those of Sunni Malikism, of Zaydism (through the Idrisids), the Shi'i Bajaliyya, and the neighbouring Bargawata, who had developed a religion of their own. The Sus had also seen the formation of *ribat* communities such as that of the Maliki Wajjaj ibn Zallu al-Lamti (whose student Ibn Yasin had become the jurist of the Almoravids), the *ribat* of Massa linked to the Gazula and the Lamta, and the *ribats* of Tit and Shakir. Some knowledge of both Islamic law and eschatological Mahdism thus existed in the area, but pagan and magical beliefs may still have predominated. Figures endowed with special powers related to the sacred played an important role in tribal societies, for example acting as intermediaries in conflicts between segmentary groups. Nowhere, however, is such a role attributed to Ibn Tumart, unlike the Prophet Muhammad.

The early Almohad movement was hierarchically structured, starting with the charismatic community formed by the companions and servants of the Mahdi as seen in the preceding section. Then followed the Almohad tribes headed by their elders or shaykhs. The tribes that joined the Almohad cause at the time of Ibn Tumart (Harga, Hintata, Gadmiwa and Ganfisa) each had a representative on the Council of Fifty (*ahl al-khamsin*) while it was operative. It was in Tinmal that Ibn Tumart proceeded to organize this Council. The names of the shaykhs have been preserved by the author of the *Kitab al-ansab* and Ibn al-Qattan, who seems to suggest that the Council of Ten was included within the Fifty. This would reinforce the idea that behind it there was a traditional Berber institution, the Ait al-Arba'in (the Forty), a council of tribal leaders. Hopkins, however, is hesitant on this point because most of the evidence points to the Ten and the Fifty being separate councils. After the purge conducted by al-Bashir, new names were added to substitute those eliminated. Did these shaykhs already hold positions of power in the tribes that adhered to Ibn Tumart's message, or did they become tribal shaykhs as a result of their commitment to the Almohad cause? Again, our sources do not allow us to reach a clear conclusion on this point. Most probably the situation was different from one tribe to the next.

Various groups were represented in the Council of Fifty. The largest was the *ahl Tinmal* (Hopkins suggests that perhaps Tinmal was already a shrine and the *ahl Tinmal* the devotees), followed by the Harga, Ganfisa, Haskura, Gadmiwa, Sanhaja, Hintata and various other tribes, such as the Lamta, Zanata and Gazula.

Among the most important members of the Council of Fifty was Abu Imran Musa ibn Sulayman al-Darir, who acted as the judge of Tinmal. His daughter Zaynab married 'Abd al-Mu'min, giving birth to Abu Ya'qub Yusuf, the second caliph. Abu Hafs Umar ibn Tafrajin – also from Tinmal – was named governor of Marrakesh and was later killed by the Banu Amgar. Yusuf ibn Wanudin al-Hintati and his brothers (one of whom, 'Abd Allah, as mentioned earlier, married a daughter of 'Abd al-Mu'min) were military commanders, while their sons and grandsons held important roles in the imperial administration up to the fall of the Almohad caliphate. 'Abd Allah ibn Sulayman al-Tinmali and Abu Bakr ibn al-Jabr al-Sanhaji were also included in the Council of Fifty after the *tamyiz*. Ibn al-Jabr later participated in the purge (*i'tiraf*) conducted by 'Abd al-Mu'min, while 'Abd Allah ibn Sulayman al-Tinmali was named governor of Ceuta, commanded the navy and executed Yaslasan, Ibn Tumart's relative. His brother Yusuf ibn Sulayman al-Tinmali was put in charge of the purge in the Gharb, the region that included both Fez and Meknes.

Under 'Abd al-Mu'min, according to al-Marrakushi, the tribes were as follows: Harga, Kumya ('Abd al-Mu'min's tribe), *ahl Tinmal*, Hintata, Ganfisa, Gadmiwa, parts of the Sanhaja and Haskura who had been incorporated after the conquest of Marrakesh, and the 'people of the tribes', which included the Hazraja and the Urika. The Haskura had initially opposed the Mahdi, for which reason they were not counted among the first Almohads. These tribes provided the troops for the Almohad army, as mentioned in Chapter 3.

'Abd al-Mu'min showed respect to the members of the Council of Fifty, who are often mentioned in his preserved letters regarding matters of concern in the empire, such as how to conduct expeditions against the Christians. The caliph employed the descendants of the tribal shaykhs in the provincial administration of the empire alongside the Mu'minid princes. The descendants of both the members of the Council of Ten and Council of Fifty intermarried, including the Mu'minid family. In this way, a thick network of religious commitment, political and economic common interests, social privilege and family connections was established among the members and descendants of the leaders of the early Almohad movement. 'Abd al-Mu'min eventually let the institution of the Council of Fifty die out.

The issue of precedence and privilege among the Almohad ruling circles was a fundamental one. In an undated letter probably written ca. 1156, 'Abd al-Mu'min explained that he had summoned all the tribes in order to incite them to read the Qur'an and study *al-tawhid*, and had divided them into three categories so that each would know their respective positions and merits. In the first category were those who had been quick to acknowledge the Mahdi, as well as those who took part in the battle of al-Buhayra. In the second category were those who had joined the Almohads between the battle of al-Buhayra and the conquest of Oran. In the third were those who had joined between the conquest of Oran and the present.

PURGING THE ALMOHADS (*TAMYIZ* AND *I'TIRAF*) AND FACING REBELLION

The tribal shaykhs of the Council of Fifty in 'Abd al-Mu'min's times carried out the 1149–50 purge (*i'tiraf*) of the Almohad ranks in the wake of al-Massi's rebellion. This rebellion had attracted some tribes in the Sus region and elsewhere to such an extent that at one point only Marrakesh seemed to have remained loyal. The caliph distributed lists of names to the tribal shaykhs and told them to make their tribesmen confess their faults, then punish them. Those affected were, among others, the Hazmira, Ragraga, Haha, Inguisat, Gazula, Haskura, the people of the Sus, of Tadla, of the region of Taza, Gumara, the region of the Gharb that included Fez and Meknes, the Tamasna, Dukkala, Haylana, Hazraja, Dra' and Sijilmasa. Perhaps remembering this purge, the caliph reminded his son Abu Ya'qub Yusuf when his death was approaching: 'The punishment for the Arabs is money and for the Berbers is the sword. Do not move your sword from the head of the Berbers and do not make the Arabs pay taxes.'

The term *i'tiraf*, meaning 'recognition' or 'confession', suggests that those who had merely pretended to be Almohads were made to acknowledge their unbelief and pay for it with their lives. Those massacred were labelled deviants and trouble-makers. Yassir Benhima has shown that among those in charge of the *i'tiraf* six were shaykhs and members of the Council of Fifty, three were Almoravids who had joined the Almohads, and four were *huffaz* (to be discussed in the last section). No member of the Mu'minid family took part, a clever move on the part of the caliph who made others bear the direct responsibility for this violent action.

Although towns such as Fez, Sijilmasa and Taza were affected, for the most part the purge took place in rural areas, targeting those

Berber tribes who had opposed the Almohads in one way or another. Some, according to Benhima, can be linked to existing *ribat*s and also to the spread of rural Sufism. In Sijilmasa, among those chosen to be killed was a pious man called Ibn Bughlat, whose prayer against 'Abd Allah ibn Watbib, the man in charge of the local purge, was said to have provoked the latter's death, enabling those condemned to be executed to go free. But elsewhere those selected were not so lucky: there were more than 30,000 victims. The women of those punished were on the verge of being sold into slavery, but Abu Bakr ibn al-Jabr al-Sanhaji, from the Council of Fifty, interceded on their behalf. Thus, peace was imposed across the Maghrib, truth reigned supreme, and differences of opinion were suppressed: this is how the purge is justified in the Almohad sources.

With the *i'tiraf*, 'Abd al-Mu'min was following a policy already initiated in Ibn Tumart's times – the *tamyiz* conducted in Tinmal in 1125 by al-Bashir al-Wansharisi. Those al-Bashir intuited as not being true believers were killed, some by their own relatives. Al-Baydhaq does not give a number of victims (70,000, according to other sources), but states that the massacre lasted for forty days and that five tribes were affected. A difference between these two purges is that the *tamyiz* was presented as the result of al-Bashir's miraculous ability to discern truth in his sleep, while in the case of the *i'tiraf* no supernatural intervention is explicitly mentioned. The Messianic element present in the *tamyiz* is substituted in the *i'tiraf* by a bureaucratic procedure in which the caliph drew up lists of names and charged a number of people with the task of conducting the operation. This difference reflects the passage from the 'mission' (*da'wa*) stage to that of the 'state' (*dawla*).

The *tamyiz* and the *i'tiraf* were not the only episodes of extreme violence carried out by the Almohads – there was also the massacre perpetrated in Tinmal shortly after Ibn Tumart settled there with his followers. At the time, an unnamed jurist from Ifriqiya who had joined the Mahdi spoke out against the killing and was executed. Ibn Tumart's depiction of the Almoravids as unbelievers made it possible to legitimize the fight against them as jihad, as we saw in Chapter 3. The accusation of unbelief (*takfir*) levelled against other Muslims had a history in the Maghrib, for example in the conflict between the Isma'ilis/Fatimids and the Cordoban Umayyads. As in some of those past cases, the rhetoric of exclusion helped the Almohads to justify the establishment of a new order, that of *al-tawhid*, which aimed at imposing a unified belief on the population of the conquered territories. The invitation to the pious Almohads to act violently against sinners is what the Eastern historian Ibn al-Qalanisi presents as Ibn Tumart's reprehensible doctrine of *takfir al-dhanb*; other non-Almohad sources insist that Ibn Tumart would order his followers to kill their father, brother or son and that they would do so, with al-Idrisi (d. ca. 1164) stating that the Almohads considered that everything was permitted to them according to their doctrine (*madhhab*).

'Abd al-Mu'min had to face some thirty rebellions in the Maghrib and another ten or so in al-Andalus. The repression of those who resisted or rebelled sometimes involved extreme violence, most especially affecting women and children. For example, Ibn 'Idhari (d. ca. 1320) describes the terrible toll of the conquest of Oran by 'Abd al-Mu'min in 1145, when many of the city's inhabitants died of thirst and all of those who surrendered were killed, adults and children. Ibn al-Athir reports that when Tlemcen was conquered after having resisted the Almohad siege, most of the men were put to the sword, while women and children were enslaved and sold.

Pragmatic reasons could determine other courses of action, as when the women of the defeated Arabs were taken captive but not sold. The sayyid Abu 'Abd Allah Muhammad wrote to the Arab chiefs telling them that their women and children were safe and invited them to come to Marrakesh to collect them; when they did so, they were treated lavishly. This serves to explain why the Arabs asked the caliph to name Abu 'Abd Allah Muhammad as his heir apparent. Among the Almoravid women taken captive in 1140–1 was Tamagunt, the daughter of Yintan ibn 'Umar, the Almoravid vizier who had helped Ibn Tumart in Marrakesh. When Tamagunt reminded 'Abd al-Mu'min of her father's actions she secured the freedom of all the captive Almoravid women; 'Ali ibn Yusuf reciprocated on the part of the Almoravids by releasing Hanwa', the wife of a member of the Council of Fifty, and the other Almohad women he'd been keeping captive. 'Abd al-Mu'min commented that they had been repaid in kind for having protected the honour of the Almoravid women. This type of anecdote is common in narratives dealing with dynastic change, as the respectful treatment of women was used as a tool for legitimization.

Occasionally, 'Abd al-Mu'min would also check his men's excessive use of violence when it jeopardized the population's support for the Almohad cause in the conquered territories. For example, when Niebla rebelled, Abu Zakariyya' Yahya ibn Yughmur, a member of the Council of Fifty, killed many of its inhabitants, showing no mercy. In response, 'Abd al-Mu'min ordered that he be taken in chains to Marrakesh, although he eventually pardoned him.

The mention of groups being annihilated, and the high numbers who are said to have perished in the purges and in conquering cities, certainly reflect the extent to which violence and cruelty were a reality of the times. However, it is also true that such exaggeration was employed as a propaganda tool by both the Almohads and their enemies, as has been pointed out by Benhima.

'ABD AL-MU'MIN'S FAMILY AND GENEALOGIES

'Abd al-Mu'min's family was itself marred by violence. His relative Ibrahim was killed by the descendant of a member of the Council of Ten, and he himself ordered the execution of his own half-brother 'Abd al-Salam.

'Abd al-Mu'min belonged to the Kumya, an offshoot of the Zanata established in Western Algeria and eastern Morocco. Among the Zanata, there were transhumant (seasonally migrating) stock-breeders, sedentary farmers and traders active on the western trans-Saharan route. From a military point of view, the Zanata were famous for their cavalry. In the tenth century, they had allied themselves with the Cordoban Umayyads and helped them in their anti-Fatimid policies, gaining local power and wealth. By the end of the tenth century, the Zanata were the masters of the central Maghrib, and to the south they held Sijilmasa. The success of the Sanhaja Almoravids was a blow for some of the Zanata, and therefore they were susceptible of being recruited into an anti-Almoravid movement. They were also suffering the political and economic disruptions caused by the Arab tribes in the central Maghrib. With regards to religion, the Zanata had participated in the Sufri Khariji rebellion of the eighth century; the Khariji Abu Yazid, who had confronted the Fatimids in the tenth century, was from the Zanata. By the eleventh century, Sunnism had become prevalent.

'Abd al-Mu'min was born in Nedroma, the area between Tlemcen and the Mediterranean, a land of mountains and woods. This was a bilingual area, more Arabized than the area Ibn Tumart had come from. 'Abd al-Mu'min's father was 'Ali ibn 'Alwi ibn Ya'la; he traced the rest of his genealogy through a woman called Gannuna, daughter of Idris II, establishing cognate descent from al-Hasan ibn 'Ali ibn Abi Talib and thus from the Prophet (see genealogical tree later in this chapter). His father 'Ali was, according to the *Kitab al-ansab*, the judge of his tribe; according to Ibn Abi Zar', he was a potter. Thus, as with Ibn Tumart, we have contradictory information regarding the social standing of the future caliph's family. 'Ali had two other sons, Yusuf and Muhammad, about whom little is known. 'Ali probably died when 'Abd al-Mu'min was young; in his journey of study, he was accompanied by his paternal uncle Ya'lu. 'Abd al-Mu'min's mother was called Ta'lu bint 'Atiyya ibn al-Khayr. When returning from the campaign of Ifriqiya, 'Abd al-Mu'min stopped in his native village to visit his mother's grave and to give gifts to his relatives, organizing a military parade with drums and banners that amazed the village's inhabitants.

During the campaign in the Rif mountains in 1141–2, Ibrahim, a brother of 'Abd al-Mu'min (or perhaps just a relative) who had just accepted *al-tawhid*, joined the caliph, who ordered that he be hosted by Muhammad ibn Abi Bakr ibn Igig. This son of a member of the Council of Ten killed Ibrahim out of jealousy for the special treatment given to him. Precedence in having joined *al-tawhid* established a hierarchical ranking among the Almohads; the fact of quartering

ARABIC GENEALOGY OF IBN TUMART AND ‘ABD AL-MU’MI

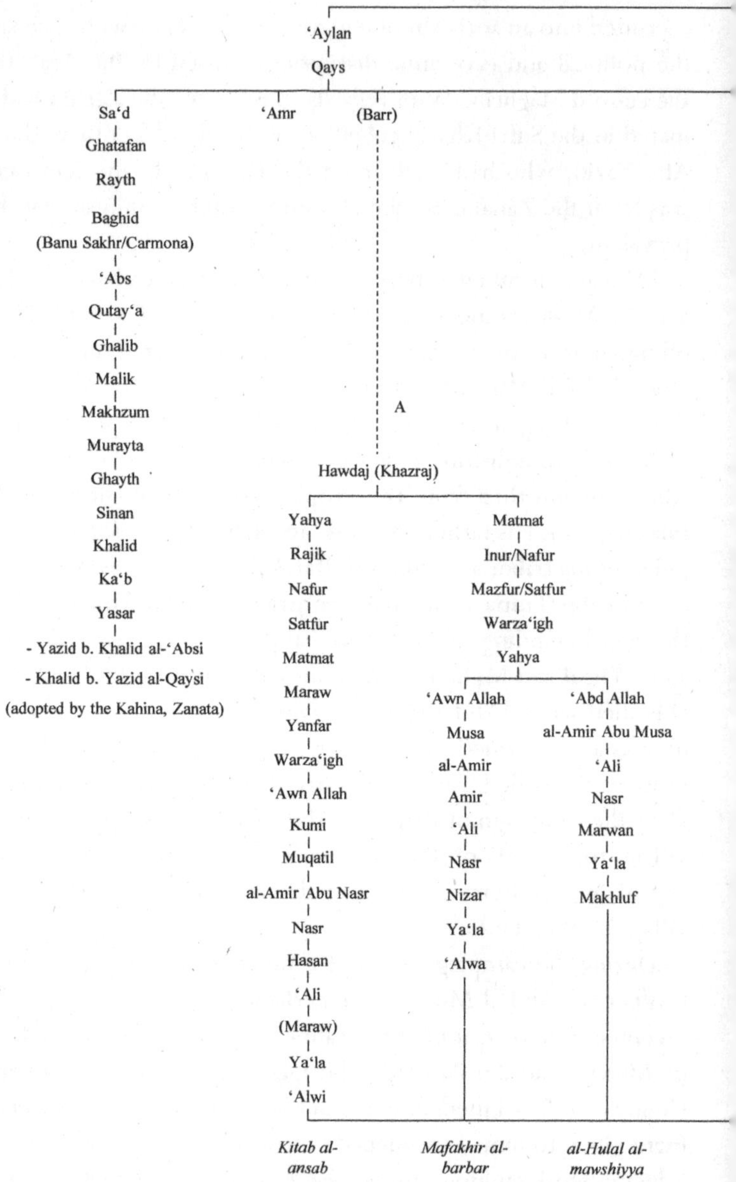

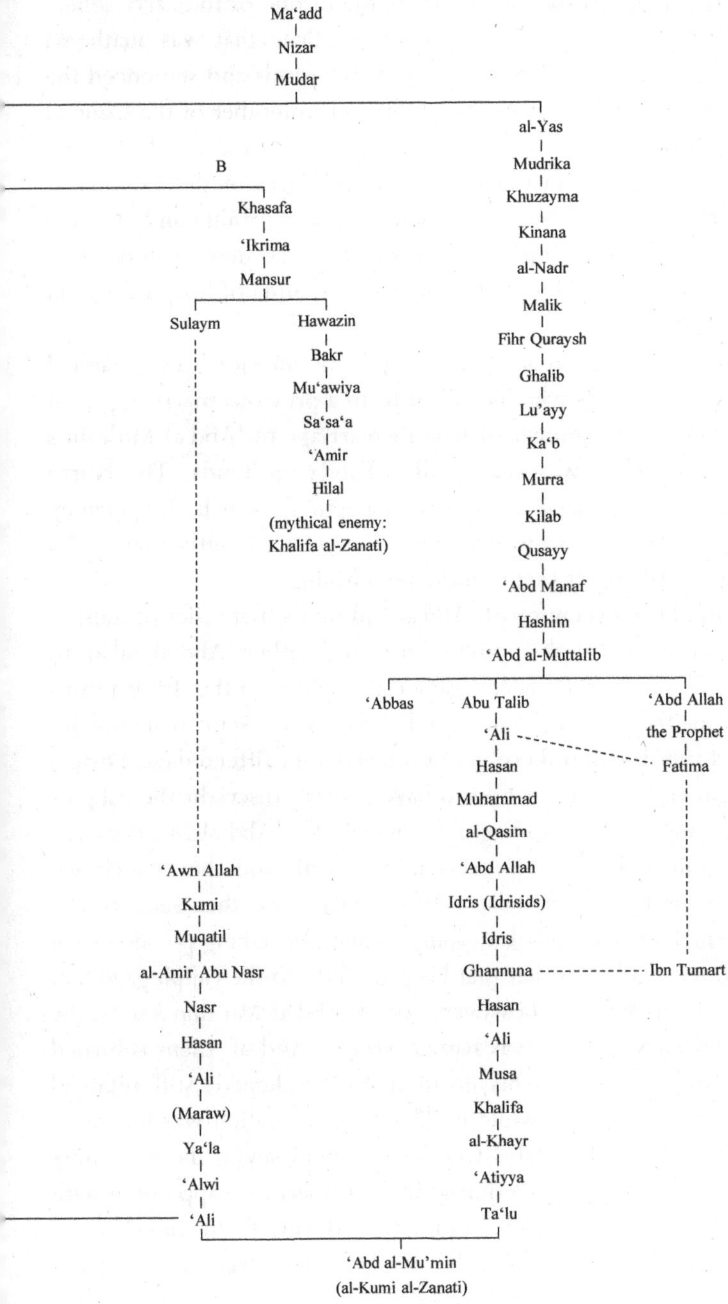
Ma'add
Nizar
Mudar
al-Yas
Mudrika
Khuzayma
Kinana
al-Nadr
Malik
Fihr Quraysh
Ghalib
Lu'ayy
Ka'b
Murra
Kilab
Qusayy
'Abd Manaf
Hashim
'Abd al-Muttalib
'Abbas
Abu Talib
'Abd Allah
'Ali
the Prophet
Hasan
Fatima
Muhammad
al-Qasim
'Abd Allah
Idris (Idrisids)
Idris
Ghannuna
Ibn Tumart
Hasan
'Ali
Musa
Khalifa
al-Khayr
'Atiyya
Ta'lu
B
Khasafa
'Ikrima
Mansur
Sulaym
Hawazin
Bakr
Mu'awiya
Sa'sa'a
'Amir
Hilal
(mythical enemy:
Khalifa al-Zanati)
'Awn Allah
Kumi
Muqatil
al-Amir Abu Nasr
Nasr
Hasan
'Ali
(Maraw)
Ya'la
'Alwi
'Ali
'Abd al-Mu'min
(al-Kumi al-Zanati)

the newly converted Ibrahim in the home of one of the early adherents (*al-sabiqun*) constituted an undue privilege that was anathema to Almohad custom. 'Abd al-Mu'min was furious and sentenced the killer to death, but Abu Hafs Umar Inti and a member of the Council of Fifty interceded on his behalf. They reminded the caliph that Ibn Tumart had given special status to the members of the Council of Ten and their descendants, promising them inviolability and granting them special privileges (all people on earth were their slaves). 'Abd al-Mu'min kept silent but had to accept the limits of his power, and the killer was set free.

When 'Abd al-Mu'min's father died, his mother Ta'lu married Muhammad al-Kumi, who had a son from a previous marriage, 'Abd al-Salam. From Muhammad al-Kumi's marriage to 'Abd al-Mu'min's mother, a daughter was born, called Funda or Bunda. The North African poet Ibn Gharla composed a poem in which the opening lines suggested an amorous encounter between the author and 'Abd al-Mu'min's half-sister that cost the poet his life.

After the 1158 execution of 'Abd al-Mu'min's first vizier (discussed in Chapter 7), the caliph appointed his half-brother 'Abd al-Salam to the post. The new vizier accompanied the caliph on the Ifriqiya campaign. After they reached Salé, 'Abd al-Salam was sent to al-Andalus to inspect the situation there, and returned after fifteen days. During the campaign, the vizier is said to have tried to discredit the caliph's sons, accusing them of leading a dissipated life. 'Abd al-Mu'min sent some Almohad shaykhs to ascertain the truth and they concluded that the accusations were false. 'Abd al-Salam was then sent to take Gabes, which he succeeded in doing, while also taking possession of all the booty, confident that that his proximity to the caliph gave him impunity. In his absence, however, one of 'Abd al-Mu'min's sons, the sayyid Abu Hafs 'Umar, was named vizier. 'Abd al-Salam returned from Gabes and, though his position had weakened, still retained some power. However, while in Tlemcen, the caliph was informed that the people of al-Andalus were complaining about the governors appointed by 'Abd al-Salam during his visit there. Disappointed with this half-brother, 'Abd al-Mu'min ordered him to be imprisoned, while making him believe that he would be soon released. Instead, while the caliph was on his way to Marrakesh, 'Abd al-Salam died in prison, with some accounts alleging the cause to be poisoning, and others a severe beating.

'Abd al-Mu'min took a wife from the Sus who bore him the initial heir to the throne, Abu 'Abd Allah Muhammad. He also married Zaynab (or Safiyya) bint Abi 'Imran Musa al-Tinmali, the daughter of a member of the Council of Fifty. She bore him Abu Ya'qub Yusuf, the second Almohad caliph, and Abu Hafs 'Umar. During his campaigns, 'Abd al-Mu'min established marriage arrangements with various groups that offered strategic advantages, as noted by Huici Miranda. After the Almohads took the fortress of Dai, the Sanhaja converted to *al-tawhid* and 'Abd al-Mu'min freed all the captives, but kept the woman who later became the mother of his son Abu Sa'id 'Uthman (who was described as being black) and possibly of Abu l-Rabi' Sulayman. After conquering the fortress of Azru during the campaign of seven years, he took another woman, who bore him his son, Abu Muhammad 'Abd Allah. The conquest of Melilla resulted in 100 captive women described as virgins who were distributed among the Almohads. 'Abd al-Mu'min cast lots with Abu Ibrahim Isma'il ibn Isallali al-Hazraji – a member of the Council of Ten – for two of them. Abu Ibrahim got Fatima bint Yusuf al-Zanati and 'Abd al-Mu'min got the daughter of Maksan ibn al-Mu'izz, lord of Melilla, who bore him his sons Ibrahim and Isma'il. 'Abd al-Mu'min also married a woman called Fatima, from Fez, who bore him Abu l-Hasan 'Ali, and a woman from the Lamta who bore him Abu Zayd 'Abd al-Rahman. Évariste Lévi-Provençal counted a total of eighteen sons from data found in the sources. 'Abd al-Mu'min also had at least two daughters, 'A'isha and Safiyya. One of his daughters was married to 'Abd Allah ibn Wanudin al-Hintati, who was killed by the Arabs in 1151 when betrayed by Ibn Tumart's relative Yaslasan. It is worth noting that 'Abd al-Mu'min does not seem to have sought intermarriage with the Almohad shaykhs. A marriage alliance with Abu Hafs 'Umar Inti is mentioned, but its exact nature is unclear.

Ibn al-Qattan recorded that 'Abd al-Mu'min closely oversaw his children's upbringing. He fed his sons excellent food, disciplined them harshly, made them learn the Qur'an, recite their canonical prayers and learn the Almohad creed, and also trained them in the arts of war. Their teacher in Tinmal was the Andalusi grammarian Ibn Mada'. Abu Ya'qub Yusuf – who succeeded his father as caliph – became well versed in philosophy. The sayyid Abu Sa'id 'Uthman was a cultivated man who supported poets such as al-Rusafi and Hafsa al-Rakuniyya, with whom he fell in love. Driven by jealousy, he was responsible for the death of the poet Abu Ja'far ibn Sa'id (d. 1163), who was also in love with Hafsa. The same sayyid is said to have ordered the death of his secretary, the poet Abu Muhammad ibn Tahir, for verses he wrote exalting the sayyid's brother Abu Hafs 'Umar.

Around 1154 – when 'Abd al-Mu'min had conquered the Hammadid kingdom, defeated the Gazula rebellion and imprisoned Ibn Tumart's brothers – in Salé, 'Abd al-Mu'min named as heir his first-born son Abu 'Abd Allah Muhammad. He presented this move as a request made by the Arab Banu Hilal, the tribes of the Central Maghrib and the Sanhaja; after consultation with the shaykhs and the *talaba*, the caliph accepted their proposal, insisting that he had had nothing to do with it. Eight years after the conquest of Marrakesh and five years after having charged the Almohad shaykhs with the general purge, 'Abd al-Mu'min profited from the incorporation of new groups into the Almohad movement to impose – making it appear to be merely a suggestion – an heir to the Almohad caliphate in the person of one of his sons. The support given by Abu Hafs 'Umar Inti was decisive, and in granting it perhaps the other remaining companion of Ibn Tumart was also showing his displeasure with the attempts on the part of the Banu Amgar to gain control over the Almohad empire by placing Ibn Tumart's family above the Council of Ten.

Abu 'Abd Allah Muhammad is said to have been deposed shortly before his father's death for his wine drinking, his faulty judgement, and even for being a leper. According to Ibn Sahib al-salat, his father forbade his name to be pronounced in the *khutba* in the winter of 1162. Abu Ya'qub Yusuf would then have been called from Seville to be named the new heir. However, Abu 'Abd Allah Muhammad seems to have ruled for some forty-five days after his father's death before he was deposed by his two half-brothers Abu Ya'qub Yusuf and Abu Hafs 'Umar. The latter was in Rabat, and was thus able to take command of the army that had been prepared to attack the Christians in al-Andalus, sending the deposed heir as a prisoner to Aghmat. At the time, Abu Hafs 'Umar Inti was fighting in the Atlas and could not stop the coup. He did, however, condemn it, as he was in favour of Abu 'Abd Allah Muhammad, whom he eventually freed (he lived until 1175). He did not pledge obedience to the new caliph until several years had passed. Perhaps he had thought he could control the heir to whom he had originally pledged obedience, whereas the new one was outside his sphere of influence.

'Abd al-Mu'min's adoption of the title of caliph entailed the attribution of Arab genealogies that can be linked to the Arabs he had defeated and incorporated into the Almohad army, as well as to the Arab genealogy attributed to Ibn Tumart (see genealogical tree earlier in this chapter). The Mahdi was presented as belonging to the Idrisids, the Prophet's descendants who had settled in the Maghrib in the eighth century, a branch of whom had settled more specifically in the Sus. The *Kitab al-ansab* records two genealogies for Ibn Tumart that go back to Hasan ibn Fatima, the Prophet's daughter; Ibn al-Qattan records three, the third being the same as the first of the *Kitab al-ansab*. The genealogy both sources have in common combines Berber and Arabic names: Muhammad ibn 'Abd Allah ibn Ugallid ibn Yamsal ibn Hamza ibn 'Isa ibn 'Ubayd Allah ibn Idris ibn 'Abd Allah ibn al-Hasan ibn Fatima, daughter of the Prophet. Ibn Khaldun, on the other hand, records two Berber genealogies and only one Arab. One of the Berber genealogies, unrecorded in the Almohad sources, is: Muhammad ibn Tumart ibn Titawin ibn Safla ibn Masighun ibn Igaldis ibn Khalid. As the Mahdi, Ibn Tumart had to be an Arab, but it is unclear when the attribution of an Arab genealogy took place (a Fatimi ancestry is mentioned by Qadi 'Iyad in the sermon he delivered in 1146) and whether it held any significance for the Masmuda or was mostly directed at the urban milieu.

'Abd al-Mu'min seems to have started using the caliphal title of *amir al-mu'minin* after the conquest of Marrakesh. In an 1147 letter addressed to the *talaba*, the Almohads and the people of Meknes, 'Abd al-Mu'min refers to himself as *amir al-mu'minin ayyadahu Allah bi-nasrihi wa-amaddahu bi-ma'unatihi* (Prince of the Believers, may God help him with His victory and provide him with His help), a formula that became standard in subsequent letters. The adoption of an Arab *nasab* that linked him to Quraysh (the tribe of the Prophet Muhammad) was needed in order to legitimize his claim to being the Prince of the Believers. This was established by making 'Abd al-Mu'min a direct descendant of the Prophet through his mother's genealogy and a descendant of Qays 'Aylan – which includes Quraysh – through his father's genealogy (see genealogical tree). In accordance with these genealogies, 'Abd al-Mu'min could pride himself on being related by cognate links to the Prophet's descendants, as well as to the Abbasids. These ancestral links also meant he was related to the Mahdi.

Among the Berbers there was a tendency to privilege female lines of descent. It is thus not surprising that in the *Kitab al-ansab* 'Abd al-Mu'min is referred to as 'the man from the Banu Gannuna', Gannuna being the ancestor that linked him to the Idrisids. 'Abd al-Mu'min's genealogy on his father's side did not go back to the direct family and tribe of the Prophet, but to Qays 'Aylan. Interestingly, among the different genealogies attributed to the Berbers in general, since very early times, they had been presented as descended from one of the sons of Qays 'Aylan, Barr, who had settled among the Berbers, to whom he was related through his mother. The Berbers would thus be Qaysi by cognate links, in the same way that the 'Quraysh' line of 'Abd al-Mu'min's genealogy was also cognatic. The Zanata were included in this genealogy. Thus, the Berber genealogy of 'Abd al-Mu'min – like that of Ibn Tumart – was only apparent, the real one being Arab; Ibn Khaldun stressed that both Ibn Tumart and 'Abd al-Mu'min had been 'adopted' by Berber tribes, which would explain how these 'foreigners' managed to become leaders within their adoptive tribes.

The advantages offered by the attribution of the Qays 'Aylan genealogy to the caliph were many: it linked him with Quraysh, as well as with the Banu Sulaym and Banu Hilal, the Arab tribes 'Abd al-Mu'min had defeated and incorporated into his army. Qays 'Aylan, moreover, was equal to Quraysh, according to the following verses: 'Quraysh and Qays are like the two legs of an ostrich: when one stands firm, so does the other.' The Quraysh had the Prophet Muhammad, and the Qays 'Aylan had the prophet (*nabi*) Khalid ibn Sinan, one of the few Arab prophets pre-dating Muhammad. The author of the *Kitab al-ansab* concluded: 'The

Qays are people of a lineage chosen for prophecy, and thus with greater reason are worthy to be people of a lineage chosen for the caliphate.' The *Kitab al-ansab* also includes predictions about 'Abd al-Mu'min's appearance, attributed to two scholars from al-Andalus – thus legitimizing Mu'minid rule before an Andalusi audience. The general import of all this is that the Qaysi lineage of 'Abd al-Mu'min, combined with certain genealogical links through cognate lines, incorporated him into a network of merit and excellence including justice, truth, militancy for God, prophecy, caliphate, conquest, righteousness, religious knowledge, generosity, respect for the pious and those devoted to religious study, and dominion over both Arabs and non-Arabs.

THE SAYYIDS, THE *TALABA*, THE *HUFFAZ* AND THE *HUSABA'*

Between 1152 and 1156, 'Abd al-Mu'min began naming his sons governors of the various regions of the Almohad empire. A letter sent by 'Abd al-Mu'min dated 1156 – but reflecting a prior policy – mentions that he had been required by the Arabs and the tribes of the Central Maghrib to name an heir; now, he said, the Arabs had demanded to be given another of his sons as governor of their lands. 'Abd al-Mu'min consulted the *talaba*, the shaykhs and other dignitaries on this matter, and all agreed to grant the Arabs their petition and to extend to other regions of the empire the nomination of Mu'minid princes as governors. 'Abd al-Mu'min took care to insist that this was not his initiative and to add that the nomination of his sons as governors went hand in hand with the nomination of a council of *talaba*, *huffaz*, jurists, judges and trustworthy men, as well as military commanders, to assist them with their new responsibilities. The government of Bougie went to Abu Muhammad 'Abd Allah with Abu Sa'id Yakhlaf, one of the Fifty, as vizier, and the government of Tlemcen went to Abu Hafs 'Umar, with 'Abd al-Haqq ibn Wanudin, another of the Fifty, as vizier.

According to other sources, 'Abd al-Mu'min's decision to name his sons as governors was presented as a request not from the Arabs but from the Almohad shaykhs. 'Abd al-Mu'min had reminded them that a new generation of Almohads – that formed by their descendants – was now trained and taking positions in the administration of the empire, and that it was unacceptable that the sons of the caliph were not likewise being considered. The shaykhs are said to have then begged the caliph to act according to what his sons deserved. In this way, 'Abd al-Mu'min transformed his wish into a negotiation, so that those who could have opposed it were now at least obliged to take it into consideration. The caliph had once again successfully managed to transform the Almohad polity, adapting it to generational renewal and to his own ambitions, while making the transformation appear to be the result of the collective will of the Almohad elites. With the nomination of an heir and of his sons as governors, the *da'wa* (mission) was transformed into a hereditary *dawla* (state). But dynastic rule, the message appeared to be, did not involve marginalizing the Almohad elites, who would retain a share of their former power.

'Abd al-Mu'min's sons were referred to as sayyids (princes). They had been given a sound education that included Arabic, and were involved in their father's military campaigns. Ambrosio Huici Miranda has noted a connection between their mothers' places of origin and the areas the sons were sent to serve as governors. For example, Abu l-Hasan 'Ali, born to Fatima from Fez, was later named governor of Fez. Abu 'Abd al-Rahman, the son of a woman from the Lamta tribe, was named governor of the Sus. Abu Sa'id 'Uthman, born to a Sanhaja woman, was named governor of Ceuta, Tangiers, Algeciras, Granada and Málaga (Granada had been the capital of al-Andalus under the Almoravid Sanhaja and before them the Zirids, who were also Sanhaja). 'Abd al-Mu'min's son with his wife from the Sus region, Abu 'Abd Allah Muhammad, was originally named heir to the throne, but the son who eventually became the second caliph was Abu Ya'qub Yusuf, born of 'Abd al-Mu'min's marriage to the daughter of a member of the Council of Fifty from Tinmal. In the first choice, his possible Masmuda ancestry seems to have been prevalent; in the second, there was a combination of ethnic and religious factors.

The sayyids are not mentioned explicitly among the recipients of 'Abd al-Mu'min's letters sent to various localities, perhaps because as sons and delegates of the Prince of the Believers they were seen as having participated in the production of the letters. From the moment Abu Ja'far ibn 'Atiyya became secretary in 1148, the recipients are – in what seems to be a standard formula – the *talaba*, the shaykhs, the notables (*a'yan*) and the populace (*kaffa*) of the corresponding localities. The term *talaba*, singular *talib*, was used to refer to the doctrinarians of the regime, seen as members of a 'corporation' more than as individuals. In the *Kitab al-ansab* – a work that reflects the 'tribal' ethos of the Almohad movement – the *talaba* are briefly mentioned at the bottom of the Almohad hierarchy. We are told they were armed until the reign of the fourth caliph al-Nasir (r. 1199–1213), and received a yearly government stipend along with other large allowances of money and clothes. According to Ibn 'Idhari, after the conquest of Marrakesh in 1147, the scholar Abu Muhammad 'Abd Allah ibn Muhammad ibn 'Isa al-Ansari al-Malaqi (d. 1178) came before 'Abd al-Mu'min, who had recruited him. The caliph, realizing that the scholar did not have clothes befitting his position, told the shaykhs that the *talaba* were naked and miserable, and that he had decided to give them money they could use for clothing and their livelihood. This allocation was maintained in later times: as the third caliph reminded the shaykhs, they had their tribes to support them, but the *talaba* did not have any other support than that provided to them by the caliph.

The *talaba*'s position as reflected by Ibn al-Qattan, who was the son of the chief of the Almohad body of scholars, is much more prominent than that described in the *Kitab al-ansab*. A distinction is sometimes made between the *talaba* and the *huffaz*. The term *huffaz* – singular *hafiz*, those who had memorized the Qur'an – can be used to refer to members of the Almohad tribes who had acquired some intellectual training. For example, 'Umar ibn Maymun al-Hargi was *hafiz* of the Jurawa; the *hafiz* Musa ibn 'Isa, charged with the purge of the Gazula, was named their governor in 1153. In many cases it is not possible to distinguish between *huffaz* and *talaba*, as has been pointed out by Hopkins. In any case, the link with the Almohad tribes was strong among the *huffaz*, but not necessarily among the *talaba*, especially among those referred to as *talabat al-hadar*.

As Émile Fricaud has shown, the *talabat al-hadar* were those *talaba* who were attached to the Almohad caliph, referred to as *al-hadar*, 'the presence', a concept common among Shi'is to refer to their imam. The *talabat al-hadar* travelled alongside the caliph: for example, they took part in the campaigns in the central Maghrib in 1152 and against Ifriqiya in 1159; they also accompanied 'Abd al-Mu'min on his 1157 visit to Igiliz and Tinmal. They were in charge of the prayers and readings from the Qur'an and the writings of the Mahdi, organized the festivities of victory, and most significantly engaged in sessions of study, debate and reflection (*majalis*, singular *majlis*) in 'Abd al-Mu'min's presence.

According to al-Marrakushi, the Mu'minid caliphs used to bring to their capital scholars versed in all sciences, but especially in speculative reflection (*'ilm al-nazar*); such scholars were called *talabat al-hadar*. They included scholars versed in philosophy such as Ibn Tufayl (d. 1185), in law and grammar such as Abu Bakr ibn al-Jadd (d. 1190), or in Sufism, such as Abu l-'Abbas al-Sabti (d. 1204). 'Abd al-Mu'min was in need of scholars who had the necessary intellectual training to give substance and conviction to the Almohad cause. None of Ibn Tumart's followers went on to become scholars of any renown or produced any works of scholarship. Their training seems to have consisted mainly in learning how to purify themselves and how to pray, and in the memorization of Ibn Tumart's creed – and this in most cases in Berber, not in Arabic. Running an empire that now included a cultivated urban population, 'Abd al-Mu'min – whose only recorded scholarly achievement was copying Ibn Tumart's *Kitab* and his commentary of the *Muwatta'* – had to seek out scholars who could offer intellectual support to his rule, especially taking into account how closely linked knowledge and authority were for the Almohads. He found some of them among those scholars who felt alienated in the society in which they lived, as if they were strangers (*ghuraba'*): to them we shall return in greater detail in Chapter 7.

The *talabat al-hadar* had a chief (*mizwar*). It is unclear if this position existed under 'Abd al-Mu'min; perhaps Abu l-Hasan 'Ali al-Ishbili, who we know occupied the post under the second caliph, had been appointed earlier by 'Abd al-Mu'min. Together with the *talabat al-hadar*, al-Marrakushi also mentions the *talabat al-muwahhidin*, doctrinarians sent to the provinces, who were of a lower rank than those in the entourage of the caliph. Both types of *talaba* were expected to study Ibn Tumart's writings and learn the Mahdi's creed by heart. 'Abd al-Mu'min needed the Mahdi to legitimize his rule: after all, he was Prince of the Believers because he was the *khalifat al-Mahdi*. The scholars who were to serve the regime thus needed to be trained in Ibn Tumart's teachings, but more fundamentally had to be closely linked to the interests of the Mu'minid family. After the conquest of Marrakesh, 'Abd al-Mu'min created a training centre to ensure the loyalty of his religious-political elites and the spread of the Almohad doctrines. He demanded from Seville, Córdoba, Fez and Tlemcen young people from reputed families, who were trained together with young people chosen among the Masmuda and his sons. The courses lasted for six months and, according to *al-Hulal al-mawshiyya*, the trainees numbered 3,000.

> He used to bring them into the palace every Friday after the prayer, and there the *Huffaz* gathered, to the number of about 3,000, all of the same age, belonging to the Masamida and others. His aim with regard to them was to train them quickly in the kind of education he desired. One day he would have them learn riding, another shooting with the bow; one day swimming in the lake he had made outside his garden... another rowing in the boats and skiffs he had made for them on that lake. They were kept at these activities sometimes with rewards, sometimes with punishments. Their maintenance and other expenses were borne by him, likewise their horses and equipment. When they had attained what was expected of them he replaced the Shaykhs of the Masamida by them in the posts of *'amil* and *ra'is*, saying 'Those who are educated are more worthy than you, so hand over your charges to them', but he made them stay with the *Huffaz* as advisers.
>
> (Translation by J. F. P. Hopkins, 1958)

Those trained were distributed all over the empire and established as groups at the service of the governors. Being literate, they were in charge of reading letters from the caliph in the mosques, thus informing the populace of significant events such as military victories. They were themselves implicated in military affairs: Ibn Sahib al-salat mentions that in 1162 the *talaba*'s names were included in the register of the army and thus received a stipend.

Some of the members of ruling families who had lost their status were are also given a subsidy, as *husaba'* (nobles, highborn people). Such was the case for Ibn Nizar, the emir of Guadix who had been deposed by Ibn Mardanish, and for Ibn Dahman (d. 1180). The latter had initially been registered by mistake among the poets because of some verses in which he had praised the caliph, but 'Abd al-Mu'min considered it an offence for someone like him who had royal ancestry, and moved his name to the register of the *husaba'* instead, granting him rents from a village.

5

ESTABLISHING GOD'S ORDER (*AL-AMR AL-'AZIZ*): HOW TO BE A MAGHRIBI CALIPH

MAHDISM, CALIPHATE AND *AL-AMR AL-'AZIZ*

According to Ibn al-Qattan, in Ramadan 1121, Ibn Tumart delivered a sermon in Igiliz in which he referred to the Prophet Muhammad as the Messenger of God, but also as the herald of the Mahdi (*al-mubashshir bi'l-imam al-mahdi*), he who would fill the earth with equity and justice just as it had been filled with tyranny and oppression, sent by God to put an end to falsehood (*al-batil*) with the truth (*al-haqq*) and to abolish tyranny with justice. Ibn Tumart continued:

> The place [for the Mahdi's appearance] is the far Maghrib and the time is the end of times; the name is the name, the genealogy is the genealogy, and the deed is the deed.

When Ibn Tumart finished speaking, ten men from among his followers – including the future caliph 'Abd al-Mu'min – openly proclaimed that this description fit Ibn Tumart himself, pledging obedience to him as the Mahdi. This scene conforms with the Weberian assertion that charisma is not so much something that an individual possesses but an attribute that is conferred upon him through the subjective perceptions of his followers. For a later author like al-Yusi (d. 1691), Ibn Tumart proclaimed himself Mahdi simply to strengthen his cause and ensure the total obedience of his followers.

Ibn Tumart's recognition as the Mahdi implied that, by that time and place, the claim must also have been made that Ibn Tumart was an Arab, not a Berber, as the Mahdi was a descendant of the Arab Prophet called Abu 'Abd Allah Muhammad ibn 'Abd Allah al-Qurashi al-Fatimi. This explains the reference in Ibn Tumart's sermon to the name and genealogy of the Mahdi. The last section of an eschatological tract included in Ibn Tumart's *Kitab* explains that the Mahdi can be recognized by six elements: his acquired nobility (*hasab*) for having established the party of the Almohads; the inherited nobility of his genealogy (*nasab*) as a descendent of Fatima; the era and place of his appearance; and what he would say and do.

We have no independent sources to check the veracity of this narrative. Thus, we can either accept what the Almohad sources tell us about the course and nature of events, or we can try to assess the extent to which those sources make sense. Why would Ibn Tumart need to convince his Arabic-speaking followers that his authority was that of a Mahdi? Had they not followed him to Igiliz – abandoning their families and their land – without such a conviction? Did Ibn Tumart address the same sermon in Berber to his Berber-speaking followers? Were the Harga and the other Masmuda likely to be satisfied having an Arab/Muslim Messiah instead of a saviour of their own? Indeed, the neighbouring Masmuda Bargawata along the Atlantic coast had for more than two centuries followed a religion brought by a prophet of their own, with their own Berber Qur'an. How did the Masmuda translate the Islamic doctrine on the Mahdi into their own language, context and expectations? How intense and extensive was their Islamic socialization?

Ibn Tumart was not only the Mahdi but also the infallible imam (*al-imam al-ma'sum*). The infallibility and Mahdism attributed to him resonate with Shi'i overtones, and scholars past and present have noted that by accepting such a characterization, the Almohads placed themselves outside what was deemed proper Sunni doctrine. Where did he take inspiration for such a claim?

A tenth-century Eastern geographer, Ibn Hawqal, had described the inhabitants of the Sus as being made up of two groups: Maliki Sunnis who were anthropomorphists, and Shi'i followers of the Zaydi scholar

Ibn Warsand. Earlier, two Andalusi scholars, Ibn Hazm (d. 1064) and al-Bakri (d. 1094), had already indicated that some inhabitants of the Sus belonged to a sect called al-Bajaliyya, which traced its origins back to Ibn Warsand al-Bajali, a Zaydi Shi'i from Ifriqiya who believed that the imamate belonged only to the descendants of the Prophet's grandson al-Hasan. Ibn Warsand converted many in the lands of the Masmuda to his belief, including the Idrisid ruler of the Sus. The Idrisids had been ruling in parts of what is now Morocco since 786–7, when their ancestor Idris ibn 'Abd Allah settled near Fez escaping from the Abbasids. The Idrisids, at least for some time, adhered to the Zaydi branch of Shi'ism. The Bajaliyya Shi'is were defeated and exterminated by Ibn Yasin, the religious leader of the Almoravids, and their property taken as booty. Those who survived became Sunnis. Al-Idrisi (d. ca. 1164), in turn, mentions that in the fortress of Tiwanwin in the eleventh century there were people who professed the dogma of the Twelver Shi'is and who were opposed to the Maliki inhabitants of Tarudant. Tiwanwin was occupied by the Almoravids around the early 1120s, around the time the Almohad rebellion began.

Despite all this Shi'i presence in the region, the Almohads never claimed any affiliation with them. With the passing of time, they tended to converge more and more towards Sunnism, to the point of renouncing Mahdism under the seventh caliph al-Ma'mun (r. 1227–1228). I have proposed understanding Almohadism as 'Sunnitized Shi'ism' in an attempt to lend intelligibility to the choices made. Ibn Tumart and especially 'Abd al-Mu'min followed certain elements and trends found in the Shi'i camp because it solved certain problems they had to face, but they adapted those elements and trends to the contexts in which they had to act, especially after the incorporation of al-Andalus into their empire, a process of adaptation that eventually precluded them from becoming Shi'is as such. It was in the early period, the most revolutionary, that we find the greater number of features close to Shi'ism, such as the use of the Qur'anic verses 28:5 and 7:137 favoured by revolutionary Ismai'ilis. These verses refer to God's promise to Moses and his people that He would turn the dispossessed into leaders and inheritors, and, for example, shows up in the title of Ibn Sahib al-salat's chronicle. Likewise, the attribution of infallibility (*'isma*) to Ibn Tumart and the use of the term *al-hadar* ('the presence') to describe the Prince of the Believers both have clear parallels among the Fatimids and other Shi'i-inspired groups.

The Almohad caliph was also considered to be the first teacher of the Almohad religious elites, a conception reminiscent of the Nizari doctrine of *ta'lim*. The Nizari Isma'ilis had emerged in Egypt towards the end of the eleventh century. Some found refuge in the West – the sources do not specify where – and from there launched military campaigns between 1131 and 1162 to take control of the Fatimid caliphate. Although they did not succeed in the Western Islamic lands, where the Almohads eventually made their appearance, the Nizaris secured strongholds in the Syrian and Iranian mountains, the most famous being the fortress of Alamut, in a striking parallelism with the Almohads' original base in the Atlas Mountains. The most famous leader of the Nizaris was the Iranian Hasan i-Sabbah (d. 1124), whose doctrine on authoritative instruction or teaching (*ta'lim*) was attacked by al-Ghazali.

As explained by Farouk Mitha, the false (*al-batil*) is what opposes truth (*al-haqq*) and the obligation exists to distinguish and choose between the two. Truth can be reached either by individual reasoning or through learning from another person, but human reason is not an adequate instrument to reach certainty in religious knowledge, as it leads to differences of opinion (*ikhtilaf*), hence only learning from an infallible teacher can truly safeguard against error. This infallible teacher must be present in the world because God would not allow truth to be concealed, and, conveniently, he is none other than the individual who publicly declares himself to be an infallible teacher, which, in the case of the Nizaris, was their Isma'ili imam. Could Ibn Tumart have been influenced by Nizari propaganda during his stay in Egypt? Was Ibn Tumart's presence in Alexandria the result of his alleged *rihla* (travel for study), or might it in fact have been related to the recruitment of Masmuda troops which began during the caliphate of the Fatimid al-Mustansir (r. 1036–1094) and continued thereafter? Did propagandists of the *ta'lim* doctrine reach the far Maghrib? A connection between Isma'ilism and the early Almohads is found in the apocryphal work *Sirr al-'alamayn*, attributed to al-Ghazali, where it is stated that the Maghribi Ibn Tumart belonged to the people of Salamiyya, the Syrian location where the first Fatimid imam-caliph had lived before moving to the Maghrib, thus suggesting that he was an Isma'ili 'Fatimi'.

Mahdism was relevant among Shi'is, and also among mystics. During Ibn Tumart's life, the Andalusi Sufi Ibn al-'Arif (1088–1141) had stated that only weak-minded Muslims believed in the need for a Mahdi to put order in the world and those who did were in fact Shi'is and infidels. Ibn al-'Arif most likely had in mind his contemporary Ibn Qasi (d. 1151), with whom he had exchanged letters and who later rebelled against the Almoravids claiming to be the Mahdi. Ibn Qasi also claimed a special knowledge of God and the occult, as he explained in his *Kitab khal' al-na'layn*, an esoteric (*batini*) work that has been shown by Michael Ebstein to be closely related to Isma'ili doctrines. Ibn Qasi was one of the first Andalusi rebels against the Almoravids who paid obedience to 'Abd al-Mu'min, later abandoning it. The coins he minted share striking similarities with Almohad coins.

Shi'i doctrines and Ibn Qasi's book leave no doubt about the cosmological, eschatological and political meaning and function of Mahdism, whereas in Ibn Tumart's case his infallibility and Mahdism – so openly proclaimed on coins and in writings – are difficult to flesh out. This intriguing situation has led scholars such as Dominique Urvoy and Tilman Nagel to conclude that Ibn Tumart's Mahdism had nothing to do with Revelation, but was instead a political move, or as Madeleine Fletcher (1992) put it, Mahdism 'simply provided the formulation of the leadership role traditionally granted by Berber custom to the holy man'. If so, as indicated above, this raises the difficult question of how the Masmuda translated the figure of the Mahdi into their own language, context and expectations.

Asking these and other questions, we can open perspectives on the genesis of Almohadism that are independent of the 'official' Almohad narrative. Such a narrative assumes there is no need to explain why Ibn Tumart was proclaimed by his followers to be the Mahdi. Thanks to this event, 'Abd al-Mu'min could subsequently claim to be the Prince of the Believers as the 'vicar or representative of the Mahdi' (*khalifat al-Mahdi*). But if we challenge the Almohad 'official narrative' we can also consider the possibility that it was the other way round: because 'Abd al-Mu'min eventually claimed the title of Prince of the Believers, he needed Ibn Tumart to be the Mahdi in order to legitimize his claim. If he was the Mahdi, Ibn Tumart's armed rebellion against the Almoravids was in fact not a rebellion at all, but a jihad led by someone who did not need to be charged with the implementation of sacralized violence by an already existing authority (which was what the Almoravids had been forced to do). Being the Mahdi meant that there was no authority above Ibn Tumart, and therefore his successor was legitimized not only in putting an end to existing rulers but also in claiming the exalted title of Prince of the Believers and passing it on to his descendants. Ibn Khaldun's discussion of Mahdism in his *Muqaddima*, based on the North African experience, underscores its crucial function in the genesis of dynasties.

Another advantage of Mahdism was that the Mahdi's successor was also legitimized to create his own religious elites, thus freeing him from the kind of dependence on the scholarly establishment that had conditioned the Almoravids. The great advantage of Ibn Tumart's representation as an infallible imam was that it allowed a specific creed to be imposed upon the population under Almohad rule – a step that Sunni rulers did not usually dare to take. The decision to do so had major consequences: it put Ibn Tumart in a position similar to that of a prophet who brought an unquestionable truth for everybody to follow, and in fact he is explicitly described as having inherited the station of prophecy.

Whatever the order of events – Mahdism-caliphate or caliphate-Mahdism – 'Abd al-Mu'min's letters and the coins he minted indicate that shortly after conquering Marrakesh in 1147 he had become *amir al-mu'minin* because of his relation to Ibn Tumart as the infallible imam and the acknowledged Mahdi (*al-imam al-ma'sum al-mahdi al-ma'lum*). This implied, as previously discussed, that Ibn Tumart was perfect in his knowledge and conduct, and that those who followed him had to obey him in absolute terms to ensure certainty in their faith and practices. In Ibn Sahib al-salat's Almohad chronicle, the figure of the Mahdi is described as he who 'stood up for God's order establishing what is obligatory' and as 'he who cured religion of its sickness and suffering'. In Almohad sermons and official letters, God's praise and the blessing upon the Prophet were extended to include the expression of God's satisfaction with the Mahdi and with the Prince of the Believers (*tardiya*).

The most striking linguistic usage in Almohad writings is the recurrent expression *amr Allah*, or *al-amr*. This is a polysemic Qur'anic term that means 'order, command, authority', but also 'affair' and 'thing'. It is not easy to translate, as it has acquired a highly symbolic, sacralized meaning because of its connection with God. In the case of the Almohads, they clearly equated God's order (*amr*) with caliphal authority and with the person of the caliph himself. Almohad silver coins include the reference to Qur'an 3:154: 'The order belongs to God entirely' (*inna al-amr kullahu li-Allah*), while the gold coins include the legend 'He who has risen to establish God's order' (*al-qa'im bi-amr Allah*) in reference to the Prince of the Believers. The *amr* belongs to God and the leader of the Almohads executes this *amr* to the extent of becoming one with it. The term *al-amr* also evokes the Qur'anic verse 4:59, where those endowed with authority (*uli l-amr*) are meant to be obeyed in the same way as God and His Messenger. This Qur'anic verse plays a crucial role in the Isma'ili religious and political doctrine that equates obedience to God and his messenger with obedience to the imam; in the case of the Fatimid imam-caliph al-Hakim bi-amr Allah (r. 996–1021) he was even called al-Hakim bi-amrihi, as the imam and God were not in fact conceived as two entirely separate entities.

In Ibn Sahib al-salat's chronicle, the Prince of the Believers is *al-amr*, qualified as all powerful (*al-'aziz*), superior (*al-'ali*), noble (*al-karim*) and happy (*al-sa'id*). All these expressions imply that 'Abd al-Mu'min knew and carried out what God had decided for humankind, His *amr*. Al-Baydhaq's 'Memoirs' reflect the crucial role of *amr* in defining the Mu'minid caliphate, as in the passage where a diviner told 'Abd al-Mu'min's mother that she would give birth to a son whose *amr* would encompass the four cardinal points, or when Ibn Tumart encountered 'Abd al-Mu'min in Mallala and told his followers: 'The *amr* upon which the life of religion depends will not come to be except through 'Abd al-Mu'min, the lamp of the Almohads.' The Mahdi also entrusted 'Abd al-Mu'min with the book with the red cover in which Ibn Tumart had read his destiny, predicting that those who would obey him would be happy, while those who opposed him would be wretched. We do not hear again of this book during the reign of 'Abd al-Mu'min, but the indication that he was now its owner was enough to suggest he had inherited its esoteric knowledge.

THE WRITINGS OF IBN TUMART AND 'ABD AL-MU'MIN

The Nasrid jurist Abu Ishaq al-Shatibi (d. 1388), when listing Ibn Tumart's innovations, noted in his favour that he never composed a Qur'an of his own. The book attributed to Ibn Tumart – known by the title of its first tract, 'The most precious thing to seek' (*A'azz ma yutlab*), referring to knowledge – is a composite work that includes a number of texts compiled with no clear overall structure. It also includes a chapter on jihad that was compiled by the second caliph. Although valuable attempts have been made to explain its contents and context, more research is needed to shed light on its sources and to compare it with contemporaneous legal and theological works.

Ibn Tumart's collected work has reached us in three manuscripts, preserved in Paris (dated 1178), Taza (dated 1198–9) and Rabat (dated 1193–4). Ms. Arabe 1451 in the National Library in Paris is presented as 'The volume that contains all the notes of the infallible *imam* and acknowledged Mahdi...according to how our lord, the Caliph and Prince of the Believers 'Abd al-Mu'min, dictated it.' The notes are said to have been taken by 'Abd al-Mu'min in the Ribat of the Harga in 1121–2, but it is not clear when exactly they were compiled to form a book or what rationale determined the book's structure. No similar 'notes' are known to have been written down by Ibn Tumart's other students, which is unusual, but then it is extremely unusual for a student to become a caliph: how could the others compete with him?

Also attributed to Ibn Tumart is a summary and re-arrangement – known as *Muwatta' al-Imam al-Mahdi* or *Muhadhi' al-Muwatta'* – of the legal work of Malik ibn Anas (d. 796), the founder of the Maliki legal school. Ibn Tumart used the recension of Malik's work by the Easterner Ibn Bukayr al-Qurashi (d. 845) instead of that of the Andalusi Yahya ibn Yahya al-Laythi (d. 849). It is preserved in a number of manuscripts; according to some of them, it was dictated by 'Abd al-Mu'min in Marrakesh in 1149 looking back on what Ibn Tumart had taught in 1121 at the Ribat of the Harga. In *al-Hulal al-mawshiyya* we are told that 'Abd al-Mu'min made the *huffaz* learn by heart Ibn Tumart's *Muwatta'*, the book *A'azz ma yutlab* and some other writings of his. Ibn Tumart is also said to be the author of a summary (*talkhis*) of the canonical collection of *hadith* by Muslim (d. 875): one of the manuscripts of this work, preserved in the library of Ibn Yusuf Mosque in Marrakesh, was copied in 1173–4 in Sijilmasa and contains texts in Berber. Our understanding of the sources, structural conception, reception and use of Ibn Tumart's writings is still unsatisfactory and in need of in-depth study.

Ibn Tumart's creed, preserved in a long version – the *'Aqida* – and in two short versions – the Guides or *Murshida*s – became the textual space in which Almohad identity was articulated. The possibility that the *'Aqida* was subject to reformulations has been discussed by Madeleine Fletcher. The uniqueness of God is the almost exclusive subject of the creed, as shown by this sample taken from the first *Murshida*:

> He is unique in all eternity; nothing coexists with Him, nothing exists outside of Him, neither land nor sky, nor water nor air, neither populated nor unpopulated world, neither light nor shadows, nor night nor day, nor reality nor noise, sound nor murmur; there is only the Unique, the Irresistible. He is in all eternity, the only one to possess uniqueness, domination and divinity. Nothing guides created things with Him, nothing shares power with Him. He has the sentence and the decision, the laud and the praise.
>
> (Translation by Madeleine Fletcher)

The spread and influence of the creed in its different versions are shown in the commentaries written by, among others, Ibn Rushd al-Hafid (Averroes), Ibn Khalil al-Sakuni (thirteenth century), Ibn 'Abbad al-Rundi (d. 1390) and al-Sanusi (d. 1490). Latin translations were also made of the *'Aqida* and the first *Murshida* in the thirteenth century by Mark of Toledo, and Castilian translations circulated among the Muslims living under Christian rule. The Almohads thus seem to have been successful in establishing the creed among the Muslim population.

The creed is generally considered to fall within the spectrum of Ash'arism, but scholars who have studied it differ in their interpretation regarding, for example, how far Ibn Tumart went regarding the ontological gap between God and the world. God is defined as 'absolute existence' and He exists in an absolute manner, which indicates a possible influence of philosophical language. The existence of the Creator-God is necessarily known by human reason. The earliest non-Almohad source that mentions Almohad doctrine, Ibn al-Qalanisi, defines it as *madhhab al-fikr*, 'doctrine of discursive thinking', perhaps precisely because of the rationalist character of Ibn Tumart's creed. Belief and devotion must be accompanied by knowledge (*'ilm*).

The longer version of the creed, the *'Aqida*, is a brief theological compendium containing a rational argument to prove God's existence and a discussion of God's attributes, ending with the mention of prophecy and its signs. The historian al-Marrakushi linked Ibn Tumart's denial of the attributes of God to Mu'tazilism, as did Ibn Taymiyya (d. 1328). Ibn Khaldun, however, denied any Mu'tazili connection; for him only Ibn Tumart's position on the infallibility of the imam was non-Ash'ari. As noted by Jan Thiele, the Tunisian scholar Ibn Baziza (d. 1264) mentions being told that 'Abd al-Mu'min would kill anyone who did not deny the independent ontological value of God's attributes, until al-Salaliji (d. 1169 or 1179), a scholar from Fez, persuaded him otherwise, in line with the Ash'ari position.

Regardless of the veracity of this story, what it shows is how problematic the original Almohad 'negative theology' was, especially because of its association with violence against those who thought otherwise. For all the Almohads' coercive power, they could not stop scholars living in their territories from thinking otherwise. An Ash'ari creed, *al-Burhaniyya*, was produced by this same al-Salaliji. This was his only work and took shape in an unusual manner. A pious and intelligent woman called Khayruna (d. 1197), who attended his classes, asked al-Salaliji each day to write a short passage on her tablet; at home, she memorized and pondered over it. Eventually she arranged for all that she had memorized to be written down. Al-Salaliji's avoidance of 'publishing' his creed himself may indicate fear of the consequences. By the time Khayruna published it, perhaps under the third Almohad caliph, Ibn Tumart's Mahdism was being eroded and the rapprochement towards Sunnism had increased.

The *'Aqida* includes a short discussion of prophecy reflecting mainstream Ash'ari positions. The *Murshidas*, directed at the population at large, make no mention of the Prophet or *hadith*, only Qur'anic passages. The first *Murshida* reflects pure monotheism, what we can call primordial *tawhid*, the essence of what the different prophets had brought to humankind. It can be said to transcend its historical actualization through Revelation. With it, Ibn Tumart was offering his followers the essential kernel of monotheistic belief, thus suggesting that, independently of what the Messengers (*rusul*) had brought to humankind by addressing other peoples such as the Jews and the Arabs, the essence of belief was simple: God's existence and unity, which was accessible to every human through force of reason. This was the message of one of the first works written under Almohad rule, Ibn Tufayl's *Hayy ibn Yaqzan*.

Ibn Tumart's representation as an infallible imam allowed for the imposition of a specific creed. This necessitated making at least the two *Murshidas* available in Berber. In the *Risalat al-fusul*, a letter sent by 'Abd al-Mu'min to the *talaba* of Bougie in 1161, it was established that the second *Murshida* had to be learned by heart by men and women, free and enslaved, and all those who were subject to legal obligations (*taklif*); without knowing and understanding *al-tawhid*, no act or word was acceptable. As regards the longer *'Aqida*, it had to be learned 'from its beginning to its last word on Prophetic miracles', including by those who spoke *al-lisan al-gharbi* ('the Western tongue'), which implies that it was also available in Berber. The author of *al-Hulal al-mawshiyya* stated that, in Ibn Tumart's time, those who did not learn it were punished with a lashing on the first and second offence, and if they persisted in their ignorance they were executed. This policy was continued under 'Abd al-Mu'min.

'Abd al-Mu'min, despite all of his alleged credentials as a scholar, did not write theological or legal treatises. Arabic verses were attributed to him and he wrote letters – or at least his secretaries did so in his name – directed to the various categories of people in his domains, communicating victories, acts of allegiance, invitation to jihad, and religious and other matters. The *talaba* read them in the mosques to expand their impact and audience. This practice was continued under 'Abd al-Mu'min's successors; previously, the Fatimids had acted similarly with their *sijill*s (official letters). More than twenty-five letters have been preserved, most of them written after the conquest of Marrakesh in 1147 when the Andalusi Abu Ja'far ibn 'Atiyya was recruited as 'Abd al-Mu'min's secretary. 'Abd al-Mu'min was the first to establish that the signature (*'alama*) of the Prince of the Believers should be personally penned by the caliph. As noted above, the Almohad caliph was considered to be the chief instructor of his religious elites, a role reflected in the fact that scholars attributed their works to caliphal inspiration and command.

BERBER AND ARABIC, IGILIZ/TINMAL AND MECCA/MEDINA

The caliph Abu Ya'qub Yusuf once inquired who had arrived at his palace and when told that they were the poet Ibn 'Abd al-Salam al-Jurawi (d. 1212) and the physician Sa'id al-Gumari, expressed his surprise at the fact that they – whose tribal affiliations proved them to be Berbers – could be cultivated men able to master Arabic poetry and medicine, saying: 'What a wonder! A poet from the Jurawa and a doctor from the Gumara!' When the comment reached him, the poet retorted: 'He has forgotten his own case! An even more surprising wonder: a caliph from the Kumya!' Having been informed of this comment, the caliph said that to prove the poet wrong he will punish him with indulgence and pardon (*al-hilm wa'l-'afw*). Regardless of the ethnic origin, the message was that it was the behaviour that made the caliph.

Moreover, 'Abd al-Mu'min knew Arabic. He came from a more Arabized area than the Sus, and had probably learned Arabic as a child, although his mother language was Berber, as revealed, for example, in an event recorded by al-Baydhaq. Rain had been falling for eight days and the riding animals had almost died in the mud; the caliph named the place where this took place as '*Tagzut n-walud*', a Berber expression used to reflect the event. 'Abd al-Mu'min spoke the Berber of the Atlas region, addressing the Harga in 'the Western tongue' (*al-lisan al-gharbi*), the language of communication among the early members of the Almohad movement (the Eastern author al-Dhahabi, by contrast, refers to this language as *al-barbariyya*).

As regards Ibn Tumart, he is said to have studied the Qur'an before he left Igiliz. Later, he was described as 'the most eloquent of people in Arabic and Berber' and he wrote three of his works – *al-Tawhid*, *al-Imama* and *al-Qawa'id* – in Berber according to *al-Hulal al-mawshiyya*. In the training of the Almohad doctrinarians in the palace in Marrakesh, the creed was taught in both Arabic and Berber. Fluency in *al-lisan al-gharbi* was required of prayer leaders and preachers. Berber was even used as a liturgical language in the Friday and festival sermons, as noted by Jones. More significantly, given its impact in the public space, the call to prayer was made using both Berber and Arabic formulas.

This concern for providing the Berber-speaking population with religious instruction in their language also existed under the Ibadis, who wrote theological texts in Berber prior to the twelfth century. Like these early Ibadi texts, the Berber version of Ibn Tumart's creed – perhaps the original text? – has not been preserved. This, despite the fact that under the Almohads a system for writing Berber with Arabic script was developed, thanks to which many Berber sentences and words have been preserved. The scholar Ibn Tunart (d. 1172) – active during 'Abd al-Mu'min's reign – compiled a dictionary that included 2,500 entries in Arabic with their Berber translations. The Berber sentences and words recovered from Almohad sources indicate that the Berber language (actually, languages; the existence of a *koine* – common language – has been suggested) had already been subject to a process of lexical Islamization. This tendency, along with the use of the Arabic script to write Berber, reveals a context of 'ajamization (writing of local languages in Arabic script) similar to others that have taken place in Islamdom, for some of which we have better sources. This is the case with the Murids of Senegal – Fallou Ngom has demonstrated how one must take into account their *'ajami* production (which has fortunately been preserved) if one hopes to understand how effective it was as a mass communication tool. *'Ajami* was used to convey to the masses the life of the founder of the Muridiyya, Shaykh Ahmadu Bamba (d. 1927), his doctrines, and the virtues he stood for – key elements in the appeal and expansion of his movement.

The use of the Berber language for religious and political communication was one of the ways in which the early Almohads showed that – as believers who had restored original monotheism – they were no longer dependent on a centre situated in the distant Arabian Peninsula. The place where Truth resided was now in the Maghrib, where the common language was *al-lisan al-gharbi*, a denomination that stressed the geographical connection and evoked the *hadith* in which the *ahl al-gharb* were described as having been entrusted with keeping the Truth. This involved a sacralization of the Berber language that transformed it into something more than a distinctive sign of the ruling elite, as had been the case with the Almoravid veil. It connected the rulers and the Berber speaking populations, proving to them that the hierarchical state that now controlled their territories was not alien to them. It drew a symbolic boundary with the East and with the other existing caliphates, most importantly that of the Abbasids to whom the Almoravids had paid obeisance. There were written versions in Berber of the caliphal letters originally written in Arabic – or perhaps the *talaba* charged with reading them publicly translated them or summarized their contents in Berber. Except for urban centres and certain areas, the degree of Arabization in the territories of the Almohad empire was low, and even nonexistent in some rural regions. This had also been the reality under the Almoravids, who were also Berber speakers, and whose lack of appreciation for Arabic poetry is often highlighted. However, the promotion of the Berber language in religious and political communications was not a feature of Almoravid policies.

The Almohads could not make do without Arabic, especially once their empire incorporated the most Arabized regions, Ifriqiya and al-Andalus. 'Abd al-Mu'min's main support came from the original Berber tribes and thus the Berber language necessarily had a place in the Almohad polity, but as Prince of the Believers of an empire that included Arabized territories and that had incorporated Arab tribes into its army, he also needed to use Arabic in a way that the original community in Igiliz and Tinmal had not. This new situation is reflected in the effort 'Abd al-Mu'min made to Arabize his sons by providing them with an Arabic-speaking tutor, Ibn Mada' al-Qurtubi (d. 1196). A grammarian, Ibn Mada' is famous for having made a bold proposal to simplify Arabic grammatical rules. This proposal cannot be dissociated from his teaching position and thus needs to be understood as having the aim of making it easier to learn the Arabic language; other efforts were made in the same direction. The Arabization of the descendants of the early Almohads who became bilingual made them more appreciative of Arabic culture.

Ibn Tunart's aforementioned dictionary was perhaps part of an attempt to establish Berber as a written language, but no grammar seems to have been produced, which indicates that for the imperial elites *al-lisan al-gharbi* was not in competition with Arabic. Writing under the Marinids who had put an end to Almohad rule and discontinued their predecessors' policies, the scholar Ibn Marzuq (d. 1379) recorded an anecdote that illustrates the limited appeal of Berber for such elites. The Sevillan doctor Abu Marwan ibn Zuhr (d. 1161) asked 'Abd al-Mu'min for permission to study Berber, which the ruler granted. And yet, after a long period of time had passed, he had only learned two words: *'awish* and *arnu*, meaning 'Give me' and 'Give me more', thus showing that Andalusis were only interested in learning Berber in order to profit economically from the new rulers. Berber could not compete with Arabic in the written sphere and as a language of prestige.

Where the Almohads succeeded was in establishing a local sanctuary. 'Abd al-Mu'min promoted the transformation of Tinmal, where the Mahdi's grave was located, into a sacred place and pilgrimage centre.

It is difficult to establish what position the Prophet Muhammad held in the religious imagination of the Masmuda. He is mentioned in the legends on the Almohad coins, where he appears as a link between God and the Mahdi – which lessens his relevance once the latter had appeared. As we shall see in the next chapter, 'Abd al-Mu'min's subjects were dissuaded from travelling to Mecca to perform the hajj, a journey that included visiting Medina, the Prophet's adopted town, where his grave is located. For the people of the mountains, it was much easier to visit Ibn Tumart's grave and other sites that had played a crucial role in his life, such as Igiliz. On 13 November 1157, 'Abd al-Mu'min sent a circular to be read out in the Friday mosques of the empire, informing people of the ritual visit (*ziyara*) that he – accompanied by the shaykhs, *talaba* and *huffaz* – had made to Igiliz and Tinmal. The aim of the journey was to strengthen the allegiance of the original tribes after the rebellion of Ibn Tumart's brothers in 1154 and the nomination of 'Abd al-Mu'min's son Muhammad as heir.

In Igiliz, 'Abd al-Mu'min undertook some construction works, repairing the cave from which Ibn Tumart had emerged to be proclaimed as Mahdi. In Islam, the cave of Mount Hira where the Prophet retired is associated with the beginning of the Revelation; Ibn Tumart started teaching parts of what later came to be collected in his *Kitab* after leaving the cave in Igiliz. But, as noted in Chapter 2, caves were also places associated with the sacred in North Africa; around the year 1000, Ibadi scholars had assembled in the cave of Majmaj in Djerba and there written the encyclopedia of Ibadi law known as *Diwan al-'azzaba*. Apart from adding a door to the cave and covering its roof with a dome (*qubba*), 'Abd al-Mu'min also inspected the construction of a new mosque. He then travelled on to Tinmal to pay a visit to the grave of the Mahdi. Al-Idrisi described it as 'a well-tended building with a high dome shape (*qubba*), but without any decoration', while the author of the *Kitab al-istibsar* described it as a holy (*muqaddasa*) necropolis (*rawda*), terminology similar to that employed for the Prophet's grave.

The development of Tinmal as a pilgrimage centre was an official decision and had little to do with popular devotion; the caliphs abstained from taking part in existing popular pilgrimages. The caliphal necropolis was established there, with the first three Almohad caliphs buried at the feet of Ibn Tumart's grave. Buresi has described the pious visit mentioned above as one of the most important ideological and ceremonial acts conceived to strengthen the imperial nature and religious dimension of the Almohad movement: it served to recall the source from which the Mu'minid caliphs derived their authority, to reinforce the bond between them and the believers, and to preserve the collective Almohad memory and group identity. The graves of Ibn Tumart, 'Abd al-Mu'min and his two successors have disappeared, destroyed in Marinid times.

THE SQUARE: COINS, DRUMS, BOOKS

As mentioned previously, the Arab Prophet is present in the legends of the Almohad coins as a link between God and the Mahdi: 'God is our Lord, Muhammad is our Prophet, the Mahdi is our imam' (*Allahu rabbuna Muhammad rasuluna al-mahdi imamuna*). Almohad silver coins include on the obverse: 'There is no god but God, the order belongs to God entirely, there is no power except with God' (*la ilaha illa Allah al-amr kulluhu li'llah la quwwa illa bi'llah*). This constitutes a summary of the basic Almohad doctrine, which makes them something more than mere coins.

The most striking feature of Almohad silver coins (dirhams) is that they are square. The square also makes its appearance in the dinars or gold coins, which are circular with inscriptions fitted in and around a square inscribed within the circle. No similar coins existed before: the new shape originated in the Maghrib and similar later coins in the East were probably influenced by the Almohad precedent. The presence of the square form was not limited to the coins: the area of command in Igiliz was also square in shape, and in Tinmal Ibn Tumart sat on a square stone in order, according to Ghouirgate, to break with the circle that symbolized the equality of those who took part in the tribal assembly. Later on, the mosque of Tinmal was built on a square plan. The Almohad troops were known for their use of square drums, and some of the copies of the Qur'an made in Almohad times were also square shaped. The square format for these copies seems to have originated in Almoravid times, but became associated more often with the Almohads. The combination of squares and circles was also a prominent feature in the decoration of book covers and flags. Thus, the square seems to have constituted something like a 'logo' for the Almohads.

Almohad coins have no date and seldom specify the mint; place names are sometimes mentioned, but their function seems to be to commemorate a conquest or other event related to that place. They do, however, mention the ruling *amir al-mu'minin*, which for the early coins makes it possible to establish loose chronologies. 'Abd al-Mu'min's successor Abu Ya'qub Yusuf is referred to as 'the Prince of the Believers, son of the Prince of the Believers' (*amir al-mu'minin ibn amir al-mu'minin*) and this continues with his son and grandson: the line of succession thus appears to have an essential, sacred quality, rather than that of human individuals. The absence of the hijra date

Almohad dirhams (left) and dinars (right) (courtesy of the Tonegawa Collection, www. andalustonegawa.50g.com/index.htm).

can be linked to the fact that the Almohad caliphate as a polity began with a Mahdi who signalled the beginning of a new age that no longer corresponded to the period ushered in with the Prophet's flight from Mecca to Medina. When at the time of the seventh Almohad caliph al-Ma'mun Almohad doctrine was abandoned, dirhams were then minted with a circular shape (with a square in the centre). Likewise, the legend *al-Mahdi imamuna* was substituted for *al-Qur'an imamuna* ('The Qur'an is our guide') and the hijra date was finally included on the coins.

Salvador Fontenla notes that Ibn Tumart did not mint gold coins because he did not adopt the title of caliph, but believes that he must have been the first to mint the square dirhams. The first areas controlled by the Almohads – the eastern Sus and the southern foothills of the High Atlas – had abundant silver mines, and the minting of coins was necessary for the recruitment, organization and payment of the troops. For Fontenla, the Almohad organization in Ibn Tumart's times would have included those responsible for the mint. Hopkins, in contrast, argues that Ibn Tumart most probably did not mint coins, as the Prophet Muhammad never did.

'Abd al-Mu'min must have started minting coinage between his proclamation in 1132 and the capture of Marrakesh in 1147, but we cannot establish the precise moment. Portuguese scholars such as J. Rodrigues Marinho have advanced the possibility that 'Abd al-Mu'min took inspiration from the mystic Ibn Qasi, who had rebelled against the Almoravids in the south-west of al-Andalus in 1140–1 and was referred to as *al-imam al-qa'im bi-amr Allah* on the coins he minted. Likewise, a coin struck in Ibn Qasi's name and dated 1144 bears the inscription *Allahu rabbuna Muhammad nabiyyuna al-mahdi imamuna*, just one word away from the Almohad inscription, where *nabi* ('prophet') becomes *rasul* ('messenger'). In these Portuguese scholars' analysis, Ibn Qasi's coins offer a less heterodox formula, as Muhammad is 'our prophet' (*nabiyyuna*), and not 'our messenger' (*rasuluna*); in the Muslim profession of faith, Muhammad is 'the messenger of God'. We lack a study of how prophecy was conceived in Almohad times that might allow us to better understand the nuances of such terminological choices.

Different proposals have been advanced regarding the square shape: it has been connected with the shape of the Ka'ba; with that of the basin at which on the day of the resurrection the Prophet will meet his community (*hawd*); and with magical squares. These and other proposals may all have something to them, as shown in Salvador Peña Martín and Miguel Vega Martín's overview article (2006). For his part, Salvador Fontenla has connected the square dirham with the shape of the scale weights used to measure the metallic content of the coin. His proposal is linked to a related issue, that of whether it is licit to mint coins, discussed by the jurist and ruler of Ceuta Abu l-'Abbas al-'Azafi (1162–1236), who quoted among others Ibn Hazm (d. 1064). This Cordoban Zahiri (literalist), highly critical of the legitimacy of the rulers of his times and thus of the coinage they minted, had stated that every Muslim should be free to carry out his transactions with bars of gold and silver, in such a way that only the weight of the precious metals would be taken into consideration, without the need for them to pass through any manufacturing process in which the original value could be altered. By using the square shape, the Almohads may have wanted to impress on the minds of their subjects that their coinage represented the intrinsic value of the metal used. Since the scale weights used to weigh coins were square in shape, the shape of these Almohad coins would have communicated their essential quality as pure metals.

Another peculiarity to note in Almohad coins is the script. Umberto Bongianino has shown how a new cursive script – Maghribi *thuluth* – was devised and used in manuscripts, funerary epigraphy, textiles, metalwork, and in coinage as a 'dynastic brand' of the Mu'minids.

THE CALIPH, PROVIDER OF HAPPINESS AND *BARAKA*: BANQUETS AND ITINERANCY

Ibn Tumart included sections on purity and prayer in his *Kitab*, but not on the alms tax (*zakat*), fasting, or pilgrimage, the 'pillars' of Islam briefly mentioned in his long *'Aqida*. A saintly figure, Abu l-'Abbas al-Sabti (1129–1204), became known for his promotion of the duty of the inhabitants of Marrakesh to give both the alms tax and voluntary alms in order to provide relief for widows, orphans and paupers. Abu l-'Abbas was from Ceuta but moved to Marrakesh at the time of its conquest, and received a stipend from the Almohad caliph – at least for a time. Perhaps it was at the behest of 'Abd al-Mu'min that he started promoting the duty of giving alms, including the *zakat* (alms tax). In his *Risalat al-fusul*, dated 2 March 1161, the caliph reminded his subjects of their obligation to pay the alms tax (*zakat*), necessary for financing jihad.

'Abd al-Mu'min is often described as spreading happiness and joy around him. The vocabulary of happiness (*surur*), prosperity (*yumn*), contentment, fortune, justice, satisfaction and abundance is prevalent in the chronicle by Ibn Sahib al-salat when dealing with his actions and presence; it also prevails in Almohad epigraphy. Positive emotions are thus associated with the Almohad caliph. Military expeditions are described as being happy occasions, even more so victories over enemies or the arrival of the caliph to a particular location. Happiness goes together with *baraka*, involving both spiritual blessing and material reward. The caliph distributed *baraka* – money, clothes, riding animals and other rewards – among the worthy. The rewarded were not only members of the Almohad elites and soldiers but also administrators, doctors, poets and scholars, among others. Manuela Marín has highlighted the dual nature of Almohad power, at the same time immediate and transcendent. On the one hand, the caliph is not hidden or veiled; on the contrary, great importance is given to his tangible presence either through his person (he commands the army, controls construction, receives delegations) or through the presence of his men (the military, doctrinarians, officials, tax collectors, preachers). On the other hand, in both epigraphy and coins, the person of the caliph disappears behind the use of abstract titles that suggest a depersonalized, atemporal and transcendent authority. He is transformed into the abstraction of his power.

Occasions for distribution of the caliph's *baraka* were victories and pledges of obedience (*bay'a*), during which the hand of the caliph was kissed; the caliph could also pass his hand over the face of a loyal follower, as Ibn Tumart had done. Banquets also formed part of the caliph's *baraka*. Communal tribal banquets were a widespread practice among the Masmuda, leaving material traces in Igiliz, where a communal kitchen has been excavated. Ibn Tumart held communal banquets with his followers and, according to Ibn Abi Zar', the Masmuda invoked his name at the beginning of every meal. Commensality was the basis of consensual links in the tribal community. Sharing food – especially the *asmas*, a traditional grain-based dish – served to settle differences and to create political and social links to enable, for example, collaborating in war against a common enemy or the conclusion of marriages and other types of alliances. Refusal to share food indicated a rejection of such contractual links. The following episode recorded in the *Kitab al-ansab* should be understood within this context. The Mahdi had attached 'Abd al-Mu'min to his tribe. After his death, the Harga prepared food and did not invite 'Abd al-Mu'min. He reproached them in Berber for their behaviour, then went away for three days; when he reappeared, he ordered them never to do it again.

With the establishment of the caliphate, tribal practices such as the communal banquet were instrumentalized in the process of state formation. Public wealth was redistributed by different means, one of them being the offering of food *(it'am al-ta'am)* that was not exclusive to the Almohads, but also practiced by saints such as Abu Ya'za (d. 1177), as shown by Francisco Rodríguez Mañas. References to banquets offered by the caliph and the sayyids are abundant: they were nourishing rulers. As a young man, 'Abd al-Mu'min had dreamt three times that the world ate off a dish which was first placed on his knees and then on his head. After having put an end to the insurrection of the Gazula and to an attempted Almoravid restoration, 'Abd al-Mu'min received in Salé the shaykhs of the rebel tribe and offered them the *asmas*. While eating it together, the caliph solemnly pardoned them and gave them his *baraka*. In 1162, having been informed of the death of his father, Abu Ya'qub Yusuf received a delegation of dignitaries who pledged obedience to him and ate the *asmas* alongside him. When 'Abd al-Mu'min took al-Mahdiyya in 1160, the victory was made public in a letter read all over the empire. The governor of Seville, the sayyid Abu Ya'qub Yusuf, offered food to the Almohads, the Sevillan elites and the permanent troops for thirty days. This practice was maintained under 'Abd al-Mu'min's successors: in 1223, Pope Honorius III absolved those Christian mercenaries who had been obliged to eat meat on Fridays or during Lent at banquets offered by the Almohad caliph to celebrate victories in battle.

In banquets offered to the army, mention is made of a special drink, the *rubb*. In Ibn Sahib al-salat's description of such occasions there is an echo of the Qur'anic passages about the rivers of wine awaiting the righteous in the Garden of Paradise. The vizier 'Abd al-Salam al-Kumi accused some of the Mu'minid princes of drinking wine, but it was ascertained that what they had actually drunk was *rubb*, which was licit; what Ibn Tumart had forbidden was specifically the sale and consumption of *khamr* (wine). 'Abd al-Mu'min, in a letter dated 1148, also forbade it, indicating that inspectors needed to distinguish between drinks that were licit and those that were not. The need to distinguish between different types of alcoholic drinks is also mentioned in the *Risalat al-fusul*, dated 1161. Drinking some kind of alcoholic beverage appears to have been widespread at the Almohad court and also more generally, as reflected in texts by Tahir al-Sadafi and Ibn Jubayr (d. 1217). Most likely, the Arabic term *al-rubb* referred to *anzir*, an alcoholic beverage mentioned by the geographer al-Idrisi as popular among the Berbers in the Sus region.

The Almohads did not develop a processional capital as the Fatimids had, but movement and mobility were nevertheless very important. As we have seen, the caliph took delight in presiding over military parades; on one such occasion, in Salé, he is said to have prostrated himself on the ground and wept. Military parades seem to have undergone a process of sacralization, becoming akin to religious processions: the troops proceeded slowly, accompanied by the sound of drums and the colours of the various banners, impressing on those who looked at them that God was on their side. This was especially the case when the troops paraded a copy of the Qur'an said to have belonged to the Rightly Guided Caliph 'Uthman ibn 'Affan (to be examined in Chapter 6).

The Almohad caliphs, starting with 'Abd al-Mu'min, were always on the move (*haraka*), so much so that their decline has been associated with the fact that they stopped moving from Marrakesh. This itinerancy was especially linked to their military campaigns, but also to the simple fact of making their presence felt, as when 'Abd al-Mu'min crossed the Straits and stayed in Gibraltar to check the construction work there and receive the Andalusis' pledge of obedience. While on the move, the caliph's presence was signalled with the *afrag*, a protective border traditionally used to guard the flock from predatory animals, but which in the Almohad case was a linen fence that set the ruler's red tent apart from the rest of the camp. This tent evoked the one used by the Umayyad caliph 'Abd al-Rahman III (r. 912–961). As Ghouirgate has noted, the *afrag* reproduced the caliph's palace in the capital; thus, when the Prince of the Believers moved, the centre of his empire moved with him.

In contrast with the Fatimids, who viewed the Maghrib as the starting point for eastward expansion, 'Abd al-Mu'min and his successors made no serious military attempt to take the Almohad caliphate beyond Tripoli. Such expansion was not needed in order to claim that the prediction according to which 'Abd al-Mu'min would rule over the four cardinal points had been fulfilled: the East (*al-sharq*) of the Almohad empire was Ifriqiya and part of what is now Algeria, referred to as *al-bilad al-sharqiyya* in the official letters.

6

GIVING SHAPE TO THE CALIPHATE: BUILDINGS, RELIGIOUS PRACTICES, LAW AND PHILOSOPHY

BUILDING THE CALIPHATE: MOSQUES, HIGH MINARETS, TOWNS AND GARDENS

Al-Dhahabi states that after 'Abd al-Mu'min conquered Marrakesh he devoted himself to construction and cultivation. Three major buildings are associated with 'Abd al-Mu'min: the mosque of Tinmal and the two Kutubiyya in Marrakesh. (He also built mosques in Taza and Igiliz.)

Construction of the mosque of Tinmal, near the grave of Ibn Tumart, began in 1148, as established by Youssef Khiyara. Christian Ewert highlights among its unique features the 'U-shaped ambulatory': the end aisles are the same width as the transept parallel to the *qibla* (the wall indicating the direction of prayer) and to emphasize this ambulatory, three *muqarnas* domes were built over the *qibla* transept at the intersection with the end aisles and the axial nave. The plan of the building is square, with the diagonal measuring 100 units. The niche indicating the direction of prayer (*mihrab*) is equivalent to one unit, and its upward projection, topped by the minaret, is included in the geometric plan, inside the perfect square it forms. In the dome of the hall before the *mihrab* there are inscriptions praising God that can be dated to the reign of 'Abd al-Mu'min.

The mihrab-minaret of Tinmal is a unique and original feature for which no satisfactory interpretation has yet been offered. It plays a fundamental role in the mathematical scheme of the building, a combination of two perfect squares and two equilateral triangles. Ewert has suggested that the precise mathematical scheme and the *muqarnas* domes, in which stars are superimposed in seven levels alluding to the seven celestial spheres, were used to represent the perfection of God's unity in accordance with Ibn Tumart's creed. The ambulatory has been related to the status of Tinmal as a place of pilgrimage in relation to Ibn Tumart's grave, and later the graves of 'Abd al-Mu'min and his successors.

Around the same time that building got under way on the mosque of Tinmal, construction also commenced on the first Kutubiyya mosque in Marrakesh (1147–1157). The Almoravids had not followed the spatial link between the palace and the Friday mosque found, for example, in Córdoba, while the Almohads revived it by building the first and the second Kutubiyya close to the Almoravid palace of Qasr al-Hajar, where 'Abd al-Mu'min resided. He included a passageway that allowed the ruler to enter the mosque from the palace without being seen, as the Cordoban Umayyads had done. A portion of the Friday mosque that had been built on a separate site by 'Ali ibn Yusuf was demolished, but it does not seem to have been abandoned, contrary to what has been stated elsewhere.

Shortly after the first Kutubiyya was finished, construction work on a second Kutubiyya adjacent to the former began in 1158. The first Almohad mosque had been considered adequate for just ten years, and it is unclear why it fell out of favour. Jacques Meunié and Henri Terrasse mention two possible explanations. One is that a larger building was needed because the population had grown; however, if this were the case, the prayer hall of the first Kutubiyya could simply have been enlarged, either on each side or by moving the *qibla* wall towards the south. The other explanation is that 'Abd al-Mu'min wanted to separate the Almohads from the rest of the population, and thus built a new mosque specifically for them. This interest in establishing a hierarchical demarcation that singled out the caliph and the Almohad elites is evident in the construction of a section specifically for them, the *maqsura*, in both Kutubiyya mosques. It was ingeniously designed, as the screen could be hidden below the floor when the caliph and his entourage were absent and raised when they attended prayer. (This mechanism has been reconstructed, and can be viewed online: http://arqarqt.revistas.csic.es/index.php/arqarqt/article/view/281)

The main reason for building a second Kutubiyya, however, seems to be related to the *qibla* orientation. In the early Almohad period there was great concern regarding this issue: after the fall of Marrakesh, for three days nobody entered or left the town while deliberations took place about whether to settle there. The Almohads were against it, and when the jurists of Marrakesh inquired why, they answered that the Mahdi had forbidden it mainly because the *qibla* of the town's mosques was not correct (the term used, *tashriq*, indicates that the *qibla* deviated towards the East). The jurists then proposed to purify the town, destroying the former Friday mosque and building a new one. But the Almohads seem to have changed their mind regarding the orientation of their *qibla*. In the second Kutubiyya mosque, the direction of the *qibla* was corrected by five degrees to the south. (Almohad mosques were oriented to the south, instead of to the south-east or east.) As explained by Mònica Rius, the method followed was based on observing the rise of the star Suhayl (Canopus) at a certain time of the year, as one of the sides of the Ka'ba in Mecca is aligned with its ascent. This is at 158 degrees in Marrakesh, and around 157 degrees in Tinmal. In Tinmal, the *qibla* of the mosque is oriented at 157 degrees. The first Kutubiyya was oriented at 154 degrees, and the second at 159 degrees, which seems to indicate a more clear alignment with the rise of Suhayl. Was this also the method followed to establish the *qibla* of the first Kutubiyya at 154 degrees? Or can we consider the possibility that the early Almohads chose a *qibla* related to their Mahdi instead of the Prophet in Mecca? This would make sense considering the strong local character of the early Almohad movement. Dolores Villalba has shown that the longitudinal axis between the two mosques is aligned towards Tinmal.

The pulpit (*minbar*) that had been built in Córdoba for the Almoravid emir was taken from the Almoravid Friday mosque and brought to the Kutubiyya, thus appropriating a highly symbolic religious artefact of the former rulers of Marrakesh and signalling the Almohads' victory over them. Marble spolia from Umayyad al-Andalus were also employed in the Kutubiyya mosques, giving them an imperial dimension.

Almohad mosques are distinctive not only because of their *qibla*, but also because of the height of their minarets. Among the minarets of later Almohad mosques the Giralda in Seville stands 50.85 m high, and Rabat's Hassan Tower, while left unfinished at 44 m, was projected to reach a colossal height of 86 m. Their precedent was in Marrakesh: the minaret of the Kutubiyya mosque stands 67.5 m tall, with a square plan measuring 12 x 50 m on each side. Gaston Deverdun, along with the majority of scholars, is of the opinion that the minaret was begun before 1158 – that is, before the construction of the second Kutubiyya – and was largely built under 'Abd al-Mu'min. No minaret on this scale had ever been built in the Islamic West. Several possibilities can be considered: the height was a reminder of the mountains the early Almohad tribes came from; it symbolized the link between God and the polity established in this world by the Mahdi; and it was a way to point to the absolute unity of God or to evoke the aspiration of human reason to reach an understanding of God extending from this world into the other.

The minaret of the Kutubiyya mosque in Marrakesh (© Susana Calvo Capilla).

Inside the minaret of the Tinmal mosque are a number of domed square chambers. For Susana Calvo Capilla, the pilgrimage rituals must have played a role in their design, although it is difficult to reconstruct their precise function and meaning. The Eastern author al-Harawi (d. 1215) stated that both al-Ghazali and Ibn Tumart stayed in the western minaret of the great mosque of Damascus, so perhaps the chambers were meant to evoke the meditative piety of such seminal scholars. Calvo Capilla also considers the possibility that the tower was designed to house the library and the two celebrated copies of the Qur'an kept in Tinmal (see below). Chambers are also found in the minaret of the Kutubiyya; in one of them, the mystic Abu Ya'za was held prisoner for a time, as we shall see in Chapter 7.

María Antonia Martínez Núñez has shown how Almohad epigraphy, whatever its location, records purely religious messages, with an abundance of Qur'anic quotations and no historical information. Art historians have long promoted the idea of Almohad disdain for artistic decoration in religious buildings, or at least a rigorist attitude in this respect. Ibn Abi Zar' recorded that when the Almohads entered Fez in 1146, the local jurists and notables plastered over the existing decorative panels in the mosque for fear that 'Abd al-Mu'min would destroy them; archaeological work has shown that such plastering did take place. 'Abd al-Mu'min would have then promoted a new aesthetics characterized by sobriety and austerity. More recently, however, van Staëvel has offered a valuable overview of the most important features of Almohad art, some of which date back to 'Abd al-Mu'min's time: subordination of plant motifs to linear and geometrical forms; formal rigour in the internal organization of religious buildings; monumentality and visual potency; and a homogeneity throughout the empire that reveals a unitary programme that should not be linked only to the political sphere, but also to the agency of those who carried it out. Van Staëvel has also underlined that the widespread idea of destructive violence against historical buildings cannot be supported by the extant evidence. While Almohad writings do not mention any intentional artistic reform, he reminds us that the tendency towards austerity and sobriety had already spread among pietistic circles, and thus the innovative character attributed to the Almohads should be nuanced by framing it within a wider context.

'Abd al-Mu'min also built towns. Moulay Idriss Sedra, for example, has argued that the caliph was responsible for the *ribat* of Taza, begun between 1153 and 1154. The construction of Rabat (Ribat al-fath) started earlier, in 1151, when the citadel (*qasaba*) including a residential palace, a Friday mosque and a number of houses was built; 'Abd al-Mu'min's two successors were responsible for the medina and the walls. A previous *ribat* had been built in the area for the fight against the Bargawata. 'Abd al-Mu'min built Rabat as a gathering place for his army before military expeditions, with the surrounding area capable of providing the necessary provisions. For Sedra, the name Ribat al-fath commemorated the victories obtained by 'Abd al-Mu'min in the central and far Maghrib, in the same way that the name Jabal al-fath given to Gibraltar commemorated the conquest of Ifriqiya. But for Sedra the main reason for building Rabat would have been to create a new urban centre for the exercise of power and to transfer there the capital of the empire, signalling a distancing of the Mu'minid dynasty from the tribes around Marrakesh and a higher degree of autonomy in relation to the Almohad shaykhs. If this was the plan, 'Abd al-Mu'min's death prevented it from becoming a reality, although under his successors attempts were made to continue in this direction, as the city's monumental – but unfinished – mosque reveals.

'Abd al-Mu'min also surrounded Tlemcen with a strong wall, ordered the construction of the citadel (*qasaba*) in Tunis, and initiated the building of a town in Gibraltar. The relevance given to such construction activities is reflected in the fact that the names of the architects responsible for the Almohad caliphs' monumental building projects, such as the Sevillan Ahmad ibn Basu (d. ca. 1188) and al-Hajj Ya'ish, have come down to us at all.

The Almoravids had done much to ensure water supply in their capital and its neighbouring areas. Ibn Sa'id al-Maghribi (d. 1274) recorded that before the Almoravids birds used to die of thirst when they flew over the lands where Marrakesh was built. The olives and fruits produced in the *bustan al-masarra* (Orchard of Happiness) in Marrakesh were valued at 30,000 Mu'minid dinars in 1148, according to al-Yasa' ibn Hazm. Some ten years later, around 1157, 'Abd al-Mu'min founded outside Marrakesh, towards the west, a great park named Shuntululya with many fountains and fruit trees; it is the area now known as the Menara, with its huge water reservoir. Its supervision was entrusted to the former ruler of Guadix, Ahmad ibn Milhan, who was knowledgeable in agriculture.

PURITY, ISLAMIC RITUALS AND THE 'UTHMANIC *MUSHAF*

The scope of the Almohads' concern for the purification of the Almoravids' misguided ways extended far beyond the orientation of the *qibla*. From Ibn Sahib al-salat's chronicle we learn that mosques such as that of Carmona were washed down, and entire cities and fortresses were cleaned and purified in the wake of the Almohad conquest. It thus appears that the early Almohads regarded the presence of non-Almohads – be they Christians or non-Almohad Muslims – as contaminating. There is a section of Ibn Tumart's *Kitab* devoted to purification (*tahara*). When Ibn Tumart went to the Friday mosque in Marrakesh, he censured the Almoravid emir for sitting on the mantle of Abu Bakr ibn Tayzmant, a piece of cloth whose manufacture had involved contact with impure materials. Two members of the Council of Fifty cleaned their mantles in the river at Tinmal: purification involved not only the body but also one's clothing. Archaeological finds have also revealed this concern for purification: in the Andalusi town of Siyasa (Murcia), founded in Almohad times, the houses had rooms for performing ablutions, a feature also found in Igiliz. Along these lines, Claire Délery has suggested that curiously shaped vessels dating back to Almohad times were portable basins for ablutions. Moreover, the Prophet, the Mahdi and the caliphs were all described as pure (*tahir*). Such emphasis on purity is, once again, a feature the Almohads had in common with Shi'ism.

Ibn Tumart's *Kitab* also includes a section on prayer (*salat*). While on campaign, 'Abd al-Mu'min and his soldiers participated in communal daily prayers, as already noted. The muezzins, equipped with instruments to tell the prayer times, were included in the Almohad hierarchical organization, divided into those who travelled with the caliph, those who stayed in the towns, and those attached to the tribes. The Almohads used specific formulas in the call to prayer that were different from those that had prevailed until then among the Sunnis of the Islamic West, and were more similar to those used by the Shi'is. Some of these formulas were delivered in Berber. One of the ways in which the caliph al-Ma'mun would later signal his abandonment of the Almohad doctrine was by suppressing such distinctive formulas. They were, however, still in use in early Nasrid Granada, as witnessed by Abu Ishaq al-Shatibi, who recorded them. Another difference introduced by the Almohads was that in contrast to prevailing Maliki practice and in accordance with the Shafi'is and Zahiris, they raised their hands not only at the beginning of prayer but also during the *ruku'*, or bowing.

The sermon (*khutba*) pronounced in the Friday prayer became especially important as new territories were incorporated into the Almohad polity. The Mahdi and the caliph were publicly mentioned and blessings were pronounced on their behalf, thus constituting a ritual acknowledgement of Almohad legitimacy that was opposed by some scholars from the reign of the second caliph onwards. Scholars who mastered the art of preaching were greatly valued by the Almohads as an important asset for changing prevailing religious practices and doctrines.

Mention has been made in the previous chapter of how payment of the obligatory alms (*zakat*) seems to have been promoted after the conquest of Marrakesh by a salaried Abu l-'Abbas al-Sabti. Abu Bakr ibn al-Jadd, the jurist from Niebla who became a member of the *talabat al-hadar*, wrote a work on *zakat* composed under 'Abd al-Mu'min or his son, an indication of its importance for Almohad financial policies. References to other religious practices that form part of the so-called five-pillars of Islam, such as the fast of Ramadan, the celebration of the Festival of Fast Breaking (*'id al-fitr*) and the Festival of Sacrifice (*'id al-adha*) start to appear from 1146 onwards and outside the Masmuda context. According to al-Dhahabi, 'Abd al-Mu'min would fast on Mondays and Thursdays.

As regards the pilgrimage to Mecca, studies by Urvoy and Jocelyn Hendrickson, among others, have mapped how it was discouraged by some Andalusi and Maghribi scholars from the late eleventh century for different reasons: to promote jihad, because of the risks pilgrims encountered along their journey, or the excessive fees pilgrims were forced to pay. There is evidence that during 'Abd al-Mu'min's reign, travel to the East was discouraged, including the hajj. Ibn Jubayr (d. 1217), who was at the service of an Almohad governor, travelled for the first time to the East in 1183, while Ibn Rushd al-Hafid (Averroes) added the chapter on pilgrimage to his legal work *Bidayat al-mujtahid* only in 1188–9. Those Andalusis and Maghribis who did perform the pilgrimage during 'Abd al-Mu'min's reign used it as a means to escape Almohad rule. The early Almohad rejection of the journey of study so closely connected to the hajj had to do with the conviction that the East had nothing to offer in terms of religious knowledge, which was now centred in the Maghrib. Moreover, the Almohads had their own sanctuary linked to the Mahdi, who represented the present, the Prophet Muhammad being the Mahdi's herald and therefore a thing of the past.

From that past came a relic that connected 'Abd al-Mu'min to the Cordoban Umayyads. The relic was a copy of the Qur'an (*mushaf*) said to have belonged to the third Rightly Guided Caliph, 'Uthman ibn 'Affan (r. 644–656), ancestor of the Umayyads. It was preserved in the Friday mosque of Córdoba and taken to Marrakesh in 1157 on the orders of 'Abd al-Mu'min. According to some sources, it had been copied by 'Uthman himself; according to others, it was one of the 'official' copies sent to the provinces; in still another version, it consisted of only four pages stained with 'Uthman's blood, as the caliph had been reading the Sacred Book when he was killed in Medina.

Ibn Ṭufayl reported that 'Abd al-Mu'min feared opposition from the people of Córdoba for taking from them the 'light' of the Sacred Book, but they were eventually happy with the transfer – how could they not be? – as they realized that the caliph was entitled to have it. The relevance of this episode has been highlighted by several scholars, among them, in the Western academic world, A. Dessus Lamare, Amira Bennison, Buresi and Travis Zadeh. It served to evoke the common Arab ancestry of Umayyads and Mu'minids, as well as the long-standing link between the Zanata and 'Uthman, the Umayyads' ancestor, at whose hands the ancestor of the Zanata had converted ('Abd al-Mu'min, let us not forget, was both Arab and Zanata). It also symbolized the transfer of the caliphate from the Umayyads to the Mu'minids, while establishing a link between a Maghribi movement, that of the Almohads, and Medina, the town of the Prophet. Most of all, it was a way to signal that God's word now resided in the Maghrib. In Buresi's opinion, 'Abd al-Mu'min was also marking a distance from the Shi'i influence that had held sway over the origins of the Almohad movement. It can be added that the Almohad shaykhs had no vested interest in such a relic: it was a 'Mu'minid' initiative that served the dynasty's interests.

According to *al-Hulal al-mawshiyya* and other sources, 'Abd al-Mu'min – and his successors – spared no expense in protecting the 'Uthmanic *mushaf*, fashioning for it a casket adorned with brocade, gold, pearls and precious gems of various colours. The casket was put in a square-shaped coffer or cabinet (*tabut*) that, when opened, thanks to a special mechanism, made the Qur'an emerge. In 1158, the 'Uthmanic copy was taken to the Tinmal mosque, and a special chamber (*ghurfa*) was built to keep it. The *mushaf* of Ibn Tumart was also deposited there, thus enhancing the sacrality of the place, surely to the satisfaction of the Almohad shaykhs.

Almohad sources give a detailed description of the rituals held around the 'Uthmanic *mushaf* when it accompanied the caliph and his troops on military campaigns. A litter (*mahmal*) with four red flags was made for it to be carried on the back of a she-camel, followed by a mule with a gold-plated square box in which Ibn Tumart's copy of the Qur'an was deposited. The camel and the mule were preceded by a large white banner. During the campaign against Ifriqiya, 'Abd al-Mu'min made the Arabs swear on the Qur'an of 'Uthman that they would obey him.

The Marinid scholar Ibn Marzuq (d. 1379) compared the Almohads' relationship with the 'Uthmanic *mushaf* to that of the Israelites with the ark of covenant. As noted before regarding Almohad art, 'Abd al-Mu'min's interest in this relic can be linked to his specific needs for religious and political legitimization, but it should also be understood in a wider context, as similar processes were taking place in other regions of the Islamic world. Thus, in Crusader times, an 'Uthmanic codex was transferred to the Umayyad mosque of Damascus in 1099 as a protective talisman. The symbolic framework for this transfer was similar, but the rituals that emerged were different, giving them a local dimension. Those initiated in Almohad times were continued by the post-Almohad dynasties; in the case of the Marinids, substituting Ibn Tumart's Qur'an with books on the Prophetic traditions.

FORCED CONVERSION: THE ABOLITION OF THE *DHIMMA*

Al-Marrakushi stated that dhimmi status had not been granted to Jews or Christians since the Masmuda came to power, and there was no synagogue or church in the Maghrib. Ibn al-Athir, meanwhile, recorded that when 'Abd al-Mu'min took Tunis in 1159, its Jewish and Christian inhabitants were given the choice between Islam or death; some became Muslims and the rest were executed. Ibn al-Qifti (d. 1248) explained that those with little to lose left, while those with burdens, families and wealth outwardly professed Islam and concealed their unbelief. In a passage found in al-Dhahabi's chronicle, 'Abd al-Mu'min explains to the Jews and the Christians living in his territories that the Mahdi had ordered that only Muslims should be allowed to inhabit them, so he gave the non-Muslims three options: convert to Islam, flee to non-Muslim lands or be killed. One group converted and another left. The churches were destroyed and transformed into mosques, and the poll-tax paid by dhimmis (*jizya*) was abolished.

These quotations are a small sample of what Muslim sources have to say on this issue. As for the Hebrew sources (on which various studies, such as Alan Verskin's, have been written), they confirm that under 'Abd al-Mu'min, Jews were obliged to convert or to leave, synagogues were demolished, Hebrew books burnt, and observance of the Sabbath and the feast days prohibited. Writing in 1148, Shelomo ha-Kohen reported in a letter to his father what he had learnt from a group of Muslim and Jewish travellers from the Maghrib: when Sijilmasa surrendered to the Almohads, the conquerors debated with the Jews for over seven months in order to convince them to convert. After that period, the new Almohad governor killed 150 Jews and the rest converted; similar events took place in other cities of the Maghrib. Musa ibn Maymun, who would later become famous as the scholar Maimonides (d. 1204), was one of those who converted until he was able to depart to Egypt with his family in 1165, where he returned to his religion. In the *Chronica Adefonsi Imperatoris*, when discussing the arrival of the Masmuda in the Iberian Peninsula, mention is made of the Andalusi Christians known as Mozarabs and the Jews who had lived in the towns of al-Andalus since ancient times, stating that the men were killed and the women, houses and riches seized.

Almohad policy towards dhimmis has puzzled modern scholars such as Hopkins, who notes – regarding the fact that forced conversion entailed the end of *jizya* – that it was 'hardly credible that the authorities would sacrifice this legal form of revenue by means of an illegal act'. This could have been what Ibn al-Qalanisi had in mind when he stated that Ibn Tumart went against Islamic law (*mukhalafat al-shari'a al-islamiyya*). I have explained elsewhere the possible reasons behind 'Abd al-Mu'min's decision – we do not know if he was following the Mahdi's orders. They include al-Tabari's legal doctrine according to which the demographic growth of Muslims made the maintenance of the *dhimma* status redundant, and the consideration of Almohad territory as a new Hijaz and therefore as a land that had to be freed of any religion except the true one. Another possibility is that 'Abd al-Mu'min was moved by the belief that all human beings possess an innate nature (*fitra*) that corresponds to the Almohad version of Islam, whereas being a Jew or a Christian depends on the family in which one has been born, which could have convinced him and the Almohads that they were in charge of the mission to bring back to true belief those born as Jews and Christians – along with the non-Almohad Muslims. The Almohad policy may also have been influenced by both eschatological and Isma'ili beliefs regarding the appearance of a Messianic figure who would bring about the disappearance of religions other than Islam, something that the Fatimid caliph al-Hakim seems to have attempted to carry out during his reign, which encompassed the turn of the century.

Active persecution, in any case, appears to have been a temporary affair. It did not apply to non-dhimmis: after taking al-Mahdiyya, the caliph granted *aman* to the Normans, who were Christians and who left the city for Sicily. 'Abd al-Mu'min's successors then had to deal with the anxiety caused by the existence of converts who were known to continue practicing their religion in secret.

MALIKISM, LAW AND THE JUDGES

The 'Uthmanic codex brought to Marrakesh by 'Abd al-Mu'min is called 'the guide' (*al-imam*) in some Almohad texts. This reflects the centrality of Revelation – the Qur'an and the Tradition of the Prophet – in the Almohads' general approach to knowledge, which went together with a mistrust or even rejection of the interpretative baggage that the Islamic community had accumulated through the centuries since the Prophet's death, including that carried out within the Maliki legal school dominant in the Islamic West.

Malikism was closely linked to the Almoravids, who had bestowed upon this school's jurists predominance over religious and legal authority. This Almoravid support, and the fact that in al-Andalus the Almohads had to confront the Maliki judges who had taken control of most cities, entailed that the Almohads could not – in principle – favour the Maliki jurists. From very early on, they also rejected their normative writings, which they dismissed as having departed from Revelation. The exception was the legal work *al-Muwatta'* written by the Medinese jurist and founder of the eponymous school, Malik ibn Anas (d. 795), as it was considered a work of *hadith*. The prestige it enjoyed is revealed by the richly decorated manuscripts preserved from Almohad times. As mentioned previously, among the writings attributed to Ibn Tumart is the summary/rearrangement known as *Muhadhi al-Muwatta'*. Maliki legal works dealing with positive law and consisting of compilations of legal questions, such as *al-Mudawwana* by the North African jurist Sahnun (d. 854), were on the other hand rejected.

A text dealing with 'Abd al-Mu'min's policies against the Malikis written by al-Burzuli (d. 1438), the Maliki jurist from Ifriqiya, has been studied in detail by A'rab. The caliph gathered a group of jurists and *talaba*, and his vizier and secretary Abu Ja'far ibn 'Atiyya told them that the caliph had been informed that some scholars had abandoned the Qur'an and the Tradition (*sunna*) of the Prophet, delivering sentences and legal opinions based on books of positive law (*kutub al-furu'*) that lacked any foundation in the divine law. Any reliance on books like Sahnun's *Mudawwana*, the vizier and the caliph warned them, would now be a punishable offence. One of the scholars present was the Maliki jurist Abu 'Abd Allah ibn Zarqun (d. 1190), who took the floor to demonstrate that Malikis were in fact following the Prophetic tradition and that what was found in the *Mudawwana* was supported by Revelation, providing arguments that supposedly won over 'Abd al-Mu'min. According to al-Burzuli, 'Abd al-Mu'min's intention at the time was to impose Ibn Hazm's doctrine. In the eleventh century, this Cordoban scholar had formulated a Zahiri (literalist) challenge to the extant Sunni legal schools, basing his approach on the rejection of *taqlid*, that is, the 'imitation' of past authorities, which constituted the backbone of the four Sunni legal schools. According to Ibn Hazm, any legal inquiry required turning directly to the revealed sources. The specific legal issue discussed in the meeting between the caliph and the scholars had to do with the proper way to repeat the prayer wrongly performed: this was precisely one of those issues on which Ibn Hazm had differed from the Malikis. Abu 'Abd Allah ibn Zarqun, according to al-Burzuli, successfully defended the Maliki position.

For Ignaz Goldziher, Ibn Tumart's doctrine was influenced by that of the Zahiri legal school and, more specifically, by that of Ibn Hazm. For Robert Brunschvig, the points of contact between Almohadism and Zahirism resided in the predominant position that both gave to *hadith*, but he has also shown that, while the Zahiris do not accept reasoning by analogy (*qiyas*), the doctrine contained in Ibn Tumart's work is not in opposition to *qiyas*, but rather to *zann*, 'probable opinion'. In this respect, Ibn Tumart departs from Ibn Hazm, while approaching the position of al-Ghazali in his legal work *al-Mustasfa*, which was summarized by Ibn Rushd al-Hafid (Averroes) in 1157 under the title *al-Daruri fi usul al-fiqh*. Ibn Tumart is, however, similar to the Zahiris in his rejection of the formula 'Every qualified interpreter of the law tells the truth' (*taswib*), although – contrary to them – this rejection of legal pluralism led him to proclaim his own infallibility.

As shown by Camilla Adang, during the Almohad period the scholars of the Zahiri school do not seem to have been agents or beneficiaries of the Almohad regime. With the exception of the third caliph, it cannot be said that the Almohad caliphs adopted any policy of preferential treatment towards the Zahiris. Even under the third caliph, however, the Maliki scholars ultimately convinced him that Zahiri doctrine was unacceptable. At the base of the Almohad interest in legal renewal was a concern with the existence of legal discrepancies (*ikhtilaf*) among the jurists. Ibn Hazm powerfully stated this problem when he asked: When Jesus appears to lead the people of Islam according to their religion, will he perhaps issue legal opinions according to a specific legal school, disregarding the others? His answer, of course, was no; there can be but one truth. 'Abd al-Mu'min's son Abu Ya'qub Yusuf showed his dislike of *ikhtilaf* in a dramatic way: when Abu Bakr ibn al-Jadd tried to explain to him the reasons for the existence of legal discrepancies, Abu Ya'qub Yusuf retorted that there was, on the one hand, the Qur'an and the Tradition of the Prophet – he pointed to Abu Dawud's canonical collection of *hadith* – and, on the other hand, the sword.

For all the caliph's dislike, Abu Bakr ibn al-Jadd's work on *zakat* – one of the legal works, together with Ibn Rushd al-Hafid's *al-Daruri*, written in early Almohad times – clearly documents the existence of *ikhtilaf*. Ibn Rushd al-Hafid (Averroes)'s legal work *Bidayat al-mujtahid*, which he started writing in 1168 (five years after 'Abd al-Mu'min's death), is also a work of *ikhtilaf*, offering a rigorous and informative overview of opinions regarding various legal issues and the reasons for their existence. He completed it in 1188, the same year the Maliki *kutub al-furu'* were burned in Fez. The caliph at the time was Abu Yusuf Ya'qub al-Mansur, who is said to have scolded the *talaba* for studying Ibn Tumart's writings instead of the Qur'an and the Prophetic traditions. Around the same time, Abu Ja'far al-Dhahabi (d. 1204), a member of the *talabat al-hadar* and expert on rational sciences active in Ibn Rushd's circle, was entrusted with the supervision of the judges and the formulation of legal opinions. The caliph al-Mansur himself is credited with a work referred to as *Fatawa majmu'a*: the Prince of the Believers seems to have been heading towards a possible legal codification with the caliph himself deciding which legal solutions were the best among those previously produced by the different scholars. Ibn Rushd al-Hafid (Averroes) was charged with laying the groundwork for this codification by collecting the divergent views in his *Bidayat al-mujtahid*. His fall in disgrace, the resilience of the Malikis, and the internal divisions in the Almohad camp would eventually put an end to this effort, such that as time passed the Almohads converged more and more with reformed Malikism.

What remained was the Almohad support for certain practices that were understood differently by the Malikis and that had to do, for example, with the raising of the hands during prayer, the sending of two arbiters when there were disagreements between husband and wife, and the triple repudiation pronounced at one time, issues I have discussed elsewhere (2005). Writing in fourteenth-century Nasrid Granada, Abu Ishaq al-Shatibi mentioned among the innovations introduced by Ibn Tumart the formulations in Berber in the call to prayer and extending the death penalty to crimes not punishable by death according to Islamic law, with a total of eighteen offences including not obeying the Mahdi's orders, being absent from three of his sermons, or denying his infallibility. As already mentioned, Ibn Tumart rejected live crucifixion, declaring the person must first be executed, contrary to Maliki practice. When the Andalusi rebel Ibn Abi Ja'far, who had held Carmona, was defeated and imprisoned in 1161, 'Abd al-Mu'min put Ibn Tumart's doctrine into practice, executing the rebel leader before proceeding to crucify him. 'Abd al-Mu'min's letters include references to legal matters, as we have seen in the case of alcoholic drinks. Concern for the misbehaviour of officials who indulged in corrupt practices is also present in some of the letters, as well as against the levying of illegal taxes and an insistence on the obligation to perform prayer.

Information about 'Abd al-Mu'min's judicial nominations is scarce. Hopkins has gathered the names of the following judges in Marrakesh:

Abu Muhammad 'Abd Allah ibn Jabal al-Wahrani; Abu Muhammad 'Abd Allah ibn Muhammad ibn 'Isa al-Ansari al-Malaqi (d. 1178); Musa ibn Sahl; Abu Yusuf Hajjaj ibn Yusuf; and Abu Bakr ibn Maymun al-Qurtubi. Ibn Mada', who moved to Tinmal ca. 1150 as tutor of the caliph's sons, later became the judge of Fez and Bougie, and during the reign of the second caliph, in 1182, he was promoted to supreme judge (*qadi l-jama'a*) in Marrakesh. In Sunni polities, judges were appointees of the rulers who in their judicial decisions were supposed to apply a law that had been formulated independently of the political power. Given the 'totalist' approach to politics and religion on the part of the early Almohads, this arrangement was substantially altered and the judges must have followed what the rulers told them to do. For most of the Almohad period there is no mention of independent jurisprudents giving legal opinions in judicial cases, and no compilation of *fatawa* pronounced in Almohad times exists, although, as noted above, the third caliph was credited with the formulation of *fatawa* and the chief of the *talaba* was in charge of controlling the judicial advisory council (*shura*).

REIMAGINING IBN TUMART AND 'ABD AL-MU'MIN: IBN TUFAYL AND IBN TAHIR

The philosopher Ibn Tufayl (d. 1185) wrote in praise of the 'Uthmanic *mushaf* and penned verses enjoining the Arab tribes to fight, reminding them of the Qaysi genealogy they shared with the Mu'minid caliph. Ibn Tufayl had himself adhered to the Almohad cause, becoming a member of the *talabat al-hadar*. His link with the Almohads was through the Berber Ahmad ibn Milhan, former ruler of Guadix, who after the Almohad conquest of the town in 1151 had moved to Marrakesh and been put in charge of the royal orchards. He brought with him Ibn Tufayl, who was also from Guadix. This was a town known for its inhabited caves and for the presence of Qaysi Arabs, the tribe from which 'Abd al-Mu'min claimed descent. Thus, the philosopher – a Qaysi – could claim to be related to the caliph and his family. Ibn Tufayl was especially attached to the sayyid Abu Ya'qub Yusuf, to whom he introduced a young Ibn Rushd al-Hafid (Averroes), in an encounter in which the Mu'minid prince showed that he was knowledgeable in philosophy; he would later charge the Cordoban scholar with producing commentaries on Aristotle. Around 1160, Ibn Tufayl wrote the work for which he is famous, *Hayy ibn Yaqzan*, known to us as *The Self-Taught Philosopher*.

This philosophical novel deals with a boy, Hayy ibn Yaqzan, growing up on an inhabited island. Deprived of human contact, he nevertheless manages to understand the world around him and eventually attains knowledge of himself and of God through reason. The arrival on the island of a man, Absal, enables Hayy to learn how to speak. Absal is from an inhabited island where he lived alongside other people, but, dissatisfied with this society, decided to leave it behind and seek out a better understanding of his own self and of God. Once the two are able to establish communication, Absal realizes that Hayy has already reached the superior understanding he has been striving for. Eventually they decide to travel to Absal's island in order to teach their fellow human beings the true knowledge they have acquired. Although they are well received by the ruler, Salaman, they soon realize that both the common people and the religious scholars in charge of spreading the teachings of the prophet they purport to follow are unable to properly understand the knowledge they have acquired. Thus, they ultimately decide to return to Hayy's island.

As I have proposed elsewhere, Ibn Tufayl's novel can be read against the backdrop of the Almohad context in which it was written. Hayy would stand for Ibn Tumart and also for 'Abd al-Mu'min, Berber speakers who in spite of growing up in areas of the far Maghrib – where urban life was limited and religious scholars were scarce and even unheard of – had the natural intelligence and spiritual drive that allowed them to grasp God's unity and understand the world. In this reading, Absal would stand for the enlightened Andalusis (such as Ibn Tufayl) who had mastery of the Arabic language, the only one suited to give proper expression to the rational and spiritual discoveries made by the founders of the Almohad movement. Those Andalusis who lived on an 'island' (al-Andalus is referred to as an island, *jazirat al-Andalus*) near Hayy's homeland were attracted by Hayy's (= Ibn

Tumart/'Abd al-Mu'min's) direct and rational approach to the Truth un-mediated by Revelation, as it echoed some of their own intellectual and religious concerns, which had made them feel like strangers (*ghuraba'*) in the society in which they lived. Salaman and his people would represent al-Andalus, a thoroughly Islamized society in which pure *tawhid* could not be followed because its inhabitants required rhetorical and dialectical means.

Hayy (Ibn Tumart/'Abd al-Mu'min) and Absal (the *ghuraba'*) also realized that to bring the knowledge they now possessed to people who were unable to grasp it was dangerous, because in the process their true teachings were bound to become distorted. Isolation from the rest of the people was the only solution. The message is clear: the Truth acquired by Hayy and Absal needed to be kept within a closed circle where only those who possessed the required intellectual capabilities could discuss it – a situation that reflects the Mu'minid caliphs with their *talabat al-hadar* engaging in debates and study sessions in which the rest were not allowed to participate.

The novel leaves open the possibility that others similar to Absal could eventually be allowed to join them on the other island, where Hayy, Absal and like-minded scholars could continue their search for the Truth, the improvement of their education and their personal betterment. Hayy and Absal's retirement from society represents the place eventually given to Aristotelian philosophy (more or less tinted by Neoplatonism according to each scholar) in the Almohad system: the caliph – with the philosopher at his side – engaged in the study of philosophy together with a few select individuals trained in the correct understanding of philosophical thought. According to the interpretation proposed here, what Ibn Tufayl's novel is transmitting are not only the limits of the Almohad revolutionary experiment, but also its continuity in a restricted context. If this understanding is correct, Ibn Tufayl was also proposing an interpretation of the founder of Almohadism that put him above and outside his original Berber context, likening him to the *wali Allah*, the philosophical mystic and the philosopher, figures that were more befitting of the Andalusi context, as shown by the examples of Ibn Qasi, Ibn Barrajan, Ibn al-'Arif and Ibn Bajja (Avempace). It is worth noting that no attempt is made to transform Hayy into a prophet, that is, someone able to put his intellectual and religious insights into a language accessible to the common folk. Ibn Tumart may have been close to the Berber Nativistic prophets in the Masmuda context, but in al-Andalus the possibility of a Berber prophet could not be accepted.

Ibn Tufayl was not the only Andalusi who reimagined the new rulers along philosophical lines. Muhammad ibn 'Abd al-Rahman ibn Tahir (d. 1178) was a member of a family of notables in Murcia who also had the *nisba* al-Qaysi, thus establishing his kinship with the Mu'minids. He joined the Almohads after they conquered his town in 1172, although he had shown an inclination towards them before. He had in fact written a tract addressed to 'Abd al-Mu'min, preserved by Ibn al-Qattan, in which he defended Ibn Tumart's Mahdism and imamate. He equated the Almohad caliph's polity to the 'virtuous or perfect city' (*al-madina al-fadila*) of the philosophers – a path that would later be followed by Ibn Rushd al-Hafid (Averroes), whose commentary on Plato's *Republic* can also be read in Almohad terms. Ibn Tahir explained that he had felt a 'stranger' (*gharib*) among his contemporaries, but when he was informed of what the caliph 'Abd al-Mu'min stood for, he realized that the end had come for the cities of ignorance thanks to the Mahdi and his successor, the Mu'minid caliph, who illuminated the lawful path in this life and also the path to the afterlife.

This interest in philosophy, which can be traced back to 'Abd al-Mu'min's time, would bear its fruits especially under the reigns of his two successors. It reflected the need of the Mu'minids for a new religious and intellectual approach to *al-tawhid* that de-emphasized Mahdism while ensuring they could still claim a superior type of knowledge.

7

THE CALIPH'S MEN AND THE REST: ADMINISTRATION AND KNOWLEDGE

SECRETARIES, VIZIERS AND PREACHERS

The position of secretary already existed in Ibn Tumart's time, but – as shown by Jaafar Benelhaj Soulami – the information we have is scant and unclear. After conquering Marrakesh and adopting the title of caliph, 'Abd al-Mu'min needed the subjects of his expanding empire to be informed that he was the Prince of the Believers. To achieve this, in addition to coins and poetry, it was necessary to produce official documents. A letter written to communicate the conquest of Marrakesh dated 1147 refers to 'Abd al-Mu'min as *amir al-mu'minin*. The skills of the unnamed secretary who wrote this letter are limited compared to those of Abu Ja'far ibn 'Atiyya (d. 1158), the secretary who wrote most of the letters (nineteen) that allow us to reconstruct how caliphal authority was formulated and conveyed. Abu Ja'far's brother Abu 'Aqil also acted as secretary, as did Abu Muhammad al-Ashiri (d. 1166), who left Marrakesh around the time of the caliph's death and settled in the East, where he entered the service of Nur al-din in 1162.

Continuity between Almoravid and Almohad times can be found in various fields, with the Banu Rushd in the legal-judicial field, with the Banu Zuhr among the court physicians, and also in the chancery. The secretaries who had served the Almoravids were sometimes kept on, as it was not easy to replace them given the long and costly educations that had equipped them with their skills. Abu l-Hakam 'Ali ibn Muhammad al-Lakhmi al-Murkhi (d. after 1184) was secretary under 'Abd al-Mu'min and Abu Ya'qub Yusuf, and his father had held the same position under 'Ali ibn Yusuf ibn Tashfin. Abu l-Qasim al-Qalami was recruited into the chancery when Bougie submitted in 1152; he may have served the previous rulers and later served as secretary to Abu Ya'qub Yusuf. Abu l-Hasan ibn 'Ayyash (d. 1173) was secretary to the judge Ibn Hamdin in Córdoba and served in the same capacity under the Almohad governors of Seville and then Tlemcen. After Abu Ja'far ibn 'Atiyya's execution, Abu l-Hasan ibn 'Ayyash became secretary to 'Abd al-Mu'min. 'Abd Allah ibn 'Abd al-Rahman ibn al-Katib (d. 1191), from Guadix, also worked as secretary to 'Abd al-Mu'min; he was versed not only in poetry and belles-lettres but also in arithmetic.

The case of Abu Ja'far ibn 'Atiyya, the most important of 'Abd al-Mu'min's secretaries, also involved continuity. Abu Ja'far Ahmad ibn Ja'far ibn 'Atiyya al-Quda'i was born in Marrakesh in 1123–4. He was the son of an Andalusi from Tortosa who had been vizier under the last two Almoravid emirs, and who was executed after the Almohad conquest of Fez. Abu Ja'far ibn 'Atiyya was in Marrakesh and managed to escape the massacre that followed its conquest. To survive, he enrolled as an archer in the Almohad army and formed part of the troops led by Abu Hafs 'Umar Inti that put down the revolt of al-Massi in 1148. When the commander decided to send a letter announcing their victory, he was told about a young Andalusi with literary talent. Abu Ja'far ibn 'Atiyya wrote a letter of great quality and when 'Abd al-Mu'min read it, he ordered that its author be brought before him, naming Ibn 'Atiyya secretary and soon afterwards vizier – a new position in the Almohad hierarchical system. All the letters from 1148 to 1158 were written by him, with the exception of three written by his brother.

When Ibn Tumart's relatives took Marrakesh by surprise in 1154, 'Abd al-Mu'min – who was in Salé – sent Ibn 'Atiyya to take care of the situation, indicating just how much he trusted him. Ibn 'Atiyya prepared a list of those who had collaborated in the rebellion and they were subsequently executed. In the year 1156, 'Abd al-Mu'min sent him alongside his son Abu Ya'qub Yusuf to Seville, and Ibn 'Atiyya took part in the reconquest of Almería, where he was put in charge of arranging the *aman*; he also took part in campaigns in Gharb al-Andalus. While in the Iberian Peninsula, his enemies accused him of sympathizing with the Almoravids. This accusation was voiced in a poem by Marwan ibn 'Abd al-'Aziz, the former ruler of Valencia who had spent ten years in an Almoravid prison in Mallorca. Although Ibn 'Atiyya had secured his freedom and brought him to Marrakesh, Marwan ibn 'Abd al-'Aziz now turned against him, with his poem warning 'Abd al-Mu'min that his vizier had sympathies for the Almoravids, who still held the Balearic Islands. Having been informed of this, the vizier returned to Marrakesh, where he was imprisoned. The next day he was put on trial in the mosque and found guilty. Shortly afterwards, the caliph decided to visit Igiliz and Tinmal, bringing Abu Ja'far ibn 'Atiyya and his brother along with him. The deposed vizier attempted to recover the caliph's favour but 'Abd al-Mu'min ordered the two brothers to be executed in a salt marsh near the fortress of Tagmart (late March 1158) on their way back to Marrakesh. According to Ibn 'Idhari, the caliph cried at having lost such a valuable collaborator.

Various factors can explain the change in 'Abd al-Mu'min's attitude towards his vizier. Ibn 'Atiyya's high position must have caused envy and the caliph may have feared the power accumulated by his vizier. The main reason mentioned in the sources relates to the fact that Abu Ja'far Ibn 'Atiyya was married to the daughter of Abu Bakr ibn Yusuf ibn Tashfin, who was also the sister of Ibn al-Sahrawiyya. This Almoravid military commander had fought against the Almohads and participated in a number of rebellions until he finally submitted in 1155. He was pardoned by the caliph and settled in Marrakesh, where he resided for a year until his loyalty was doubted and the caliph decided to imprison him. Abu Ja'far ibn 'Atiyya informed his brother-in-law through his wife of the caliph's intentions, advising him to pretend to be sick and use the time thus gained to escape, seeking refuge with the Banu Ghaniya in Mallorca. Ibn al-Sahrawiyya was imprudent enough to tell this to a friend, who betrayed him.

Thus Abu Ja'far ibn 'Atiyya chose loyalty to his kin above loyalty to the caliph, and was eventually executed, as mentioned above. It is notable, however, that his past at the service of the Almoravids and his family connections with them had not previously been taken into account. Moreover, the fact that 'Abd al-Mu'min did not execute him at once but took him along on his visit to the sites associated with Ibn Tumart's life, only to then proceed with his execution, may indicate that Ibn 'Atiyya's fall from grace had to do with his decisive intervention in executing Ibn Tumart's brothers and those who had joined them, with all probability members of the Harga tribe. 'Abd al-Mu'min's visit to Igiliz – and the construction he undertook there – and Tinmal would therefore have been a way to mend his relations with the Harga and the original Almohad tribes. In my view, 'Abd al-Mu'min brought Ibn 'Atiyya along on this journey in order to parade the person responsible for the death of Ibn Tumart's brothers, and his ensuing execution was a way to regain the Harga's allegiance.

After the fall of the Banu 'Atiyya, 'Abd al-Mu'min named his step-brother 'Abd al-Salam al-Kumi, whose trajectory and eventual death was discussed in Chapter 4, as vizier. After him, the sayyid Abu Hafs was named vizier and continued as such when his brother Abu Ya'qub Yusuf succeeded 'Abd al-Mu'min. Acting as the vizier's second in command was Abu l-Ula Idris ibn Jami', the son of one of the members of the *ahl al-dar* mentioned in Chapter 4. Abu l-Ula grew up in the caliph's palace and his intimate relationship with the Mu'minids led him to be chosen as 'vice' vizier – probably the one who actually did all the work. According to Hopkins, the Almohad vizier was merely an executive functionary without the power to make independent decisions; thus, whenever the caliph left on a campaign, it was a sayyid rather than the vizier who was left as his deputy. After the fall of the Banu 'Atiyya, only members close to the caliph or to the early Almohads were named viziers.

As mentioned in the previous chapter, Ibn Tumart had decreed the death penalty for those who missed three or more of his sermons and for those officials, including preachers, who failed to memorize and publicly profess the creed. Ibn Tumart's preachers, called *mubashshirun*, had been entrusted, according to al-Marrakushi, with the task of spreading his message in order to win over the heads of the tribes. Under 'Abd al-Mu'min, the preachers were in charge of delivering the sermon in the Friday mosques and on other occasions, such as the ceremonies held whenever a region accepted Almohad rule.

The judge 'Abd Allah ibn Jabal al-Wahrani – whose family from al-Andalus had settled in Oran – was a preacher greatly honoured by the caliph. He died in Marrakesh in 1162 and was buried in the cemetery known as Rawdat al-shuyukh. Another Andalusi scholar, Abu Bakr ibn al-Jadd, delivered a sermon in Salé in April 1151 in which he made an invocation (*du'a'*) for the caliph and extolled the duty of rushing to obey him; the Andalusi delegates from Carmona and Córdoba then proclaimed the oath of loyalty to 'Abd al-Mu'min. Abu l-Hasan al-Ishbili al-Usuli was a specialist on Ash'ari theology who had approached 'Abd al-Mu'min when he was besieging Aghmat and presented him his book entitled *al-Mi'raj* (which has unfortunately been lost). He then settled in Marrakesh, where he taught Ibn Tumart's works. Lastly, we might mention Abu Muhammad 'Abd Allah ibn Muhammad ibn 'Isa al-Ansari al-Malaqi (d. 1178), a student of the mystic Ibn Barrajan who became the head of the *talabat al-hadar* under the second caliph.

POETS, HISTORIANS AND GRAMMARIANS

Did the Masmuda have a poetic tradition of their own that they used to praise their Mahdi? This we do not know, but as regards Arabic poetry, it is absent in the early Almohad period. After the conquest of Marrakesh, it appears as one of the means through which the caliph publicized his victories and achievements, and also as one of the means through which his exalted role of Prince of the Believers was acknowledged. Some verses, translated by Rachid Bourouiba, are even attributed to 'Abd al-Mu'min himself.

Poetry and politics have always been closely linked in Arab culture. During the Almoravid period, the Andalusi poets had complained that the Sanhaja rulers had forsaken one of the functions of power. With the arrival of the Almohad caliph in Gibraltar in 1160 to inspect the situation in al-Andalus, poetry regained its former political function. An audience was organized to receive the delegations that arrived from the different regions to pledge obedience. The caliph rewarded the poems composed for the occasion. Teresa Garulo has shown how the poems recited there aimed at creating a link with previous caliphates, mainly the Umayyad but also the Fatimid: thus the poet Ibn Habus from Fez (1106–1174) was compared to Ibn Hani', the panegyrist of the Fatimids, and another poet was said to be the descendant of a famous Cordoban Umayyad poet.

The event also aimed to demonstrate that 'Abd al-Mu'min was able to understand the Arabic poems, in contrast to Yusuf ibn Tashfin who had been unable to make sense of the verses quoted by the Taifa king of Seville al-Mu'tamid when he had called on the Almoravid emir for help. 'Abd al-Mu'min was even able to voice his criticism of some of the poems, thus proving himself to be a cultivated ruler. The Berber North African poet al-Jurawi was praised by 'Abd al-Mu'min, who said: 'Oh, Abu l-'Abbas, with you we can compete with the Andalusis.' Al-Jurawi mostly wrote panegyrics of the first three Almohad caliphs, but also an anthology of Arabic poems – known as *al-Hamasa al-maghribiyya* – in emulation of the famous *Hamasa* of the Arab poet Abu Tammam (d. 846). The verses recited by al-Rusafi from Valencia (d. 1177) illustrated Almohad self-representation, mentioning the light of prophecy and good guidance and the Arabic genealogy claimed by 'Abd al-Mu'min, whose purity and sanctity were also praised. Reference was made to Gibraltar as the place where two seas unite in the story of Moses (Qur'an 18:59–60), with Ibn Tumart compared to Moses and 'Abd al-Mu'min to Joshua. The caliph was also compared to Musa ibn Nusayr and Tariq ibn Ziyad, the conquerors of al-Andalus.

Women also wrote poetry honouring the caliph, among them Asma' al-'Amiriyya, mentioned in the Introduction. A cultivated slave called al-'Alya' al-Balansiyya stated in her verses that the caliph 'shows us how imperfect we normal creatures are'. As we have seen, 'Abd al-Mu'min was especially generous with the poet Hafsa al-Rakuniyya, to whom he entrusted his daughters' education.

The caliph established a register of salaried poets. As noted by Garulo, when reciting panegyrics, especially in public audiences, the poet acted as the representative of the community in front of the ruler. The solemn recitation of the poem was an act of collective affirmation of loyalty, and also a reminder of the ideals that the ruler represented. The economic reward given to the poet proved the superiority of the panegyric's addressee and also the veracity of the poem. The Almohad rulers often ordered that a poem be preserved or memorized, as happened with the letter containing verses with which 'Abd al-Mu'min communicated the conquest of al-Mahdiyya to the Andalusis.

Given that panegyric poetry was a powerful means of legitimization, it was usually quoted in official chronicles. That is the case with the panegyric written by Ibn Sahib al-salat (d. after 1197) from Beja (southern Portugal), who joined the Almohads around 1162, shortly before 'Abd al-Mu'min's death. He became a member of the entourage of the sayyid Abu Sa'id as one of the *talaba* and visited Marrakesh, where he studied several key Almohad texts. His chronicle is entitled '[Divine] gift of the imamate given to those who had been previously humiliated, as God has made them the rightful leaders (imams) and has made them inheritors [of their oppressors]' (*al-Mann bi'l-imama 'ala l-mustad'afin bi-an ja'alahum Allah a'imma wa-ja'alahum al-warithin*), a title based on Qur'an 28:5, which promises to Moses and his people a reversal of the existing order. Only a fragment has been preserved of his chronicle, valuable not only because of its information on military and political events, but especially because of the highly charged and elaborate propagandistic language used to exalt the Mu'minid caliphs, as studied by Marín, and to demonize their enemies, as studied by Jones. The ruler of Murcia Ibn Mardanish and his father-in-law Ibn Hamushk were especially targeted because of their lengthy resistance to the Almohads.

Manuel Acién has called attention to the unprecedented level of sycophancy developed by pro-Almohad historians, Ibn Sahib al-salat's chronicle being a case in point. Another example is the poem written by Abu Ja'far ibn Sa'id in which he justified the imprisonment of his own father, the ruler of Alcalá la Real, at the hands of 'Abd al-Mu'min, even telling his father that he should be happy for his lot:

> My lord, if the best caliph imprisoned you this is for you an honour and involves great prestige.

The Marinid historian Ibn Abi Zar' (d. between 1310 and 1320) described 'Abd al-Mu'min as versed in history and in the wars of the peoples. Certainly, in order to consolidate his power, 'Abd al-Mu'min understood the need to generate a historiographical record offering a version of Almohad history that suited his interests. This is what we find in al-Baydhaq's 'Memoirs', of which the first part, dealing with Ibn Tumart's earliest life stages, is lost; what has been preserved starts with Ibn Tumart's arrival in Tunis. Al-Baydhaq claims to have been an early follower of Ibn Tumart who joined him in Tripoli and accompanied him until his death, having been present in the events he describes, but we have no independent evidence of his existence apart from his own writing. Critical analysis reveals inconsistencies that shed doubt on the claims he makes. As highlighted by Victoria Aguilar and Loïc Bombrun, al-Baydhaq's narrative is aimed at proving that 'Abd al-Mu'min was chosen by Ibn Tumart as his favourite student and to convey the inevitability of his succession to the Mahdi. The autobiographical character of this work – whether real or alleged – is reminiscent of the autobiographies written by followers of the early Fatimid caliphs in which they recorded the services they rendered to the dynasty.

Another scholar who wrote history at the service of 'Abd al-Mu'min was Abu 'Ali Hasan ibn 'Abd Allah ibn al-Ashiri (d. after 1173) from Tlemcen, where he was living at the time of its conquest by the Almohads in 1145. He attached himself to 'Abd al-Mu'min, writing verses in his honour and a work, now lost, entitled 'Arrangement of pearls on the conquests by the High Order' (*Nazm al-la'ali fi futuh al-amr al-'ali*). The Andalusi scholar and poet Muhammad ibn 'Umar al-Shawwash al-Shilbi (d. 1174) is credited with a (lost) work on Ibn Qasi's rebellion, perhaps a confusion with that attributed to Ibn Sahib al-salat, which in any case reveals the interest that the mystic elicited in 'Abd al-Mu'min's court. Al-Shawwash wrote verses on the occasion of the sayyid Muhammad's nomination as heir, and also when he was proclaimed caliph in Salé. To Ahmad ibn 'Abd al-Samad al-Khazraji al-Qurtubi (d. 1187) is attributed a voluminous book starting with Creation and ending with the reign of 'Abd al-Mu'min. It is unfortunate that it has not been preserved, as it would have shed light on how this scholar positioned the Almohads within the framework of universal history. Ibn 'Abd al-Samad left al-Andalus after having spent some years in Christian Toledo and settled in Fez, where he taught *hadith* in al-Qarawiyyin mosque.

The historical works so far reviewed were all pro-Almohad. Special cases are the following two works written by historians who had first hand knowledge of 'Abd al-Mu'min's times but whose adherence to *al-tawhid* is unclear. Al-Yasa' ibn Hazm (d. 1179) was a scholar from al-Andalus who resided for a time in Murcia, where he was secretary of the rulers who took control after the Almoravid collapse. In 1148, according to his own testimony, he was in Marrakesh, but we do not know in what capacity. In 1164, he travelled to the East and never returned to al-Andalus. He arrived in Egypt when it was still under Fatimid rule, but in 1171 the Ayyubid sultan Saladin proclaimed a return to 'Abbasid obedience. Al-Yasa' entered into his service, receiving a monthly stipend after becoming the first who dared to pronounce the Friday sermon in Cairo in the name of the 'Abbasids. Saladin charged him with writing a history of the Maghrib which is lost, but extensive quotations have been preserved by later authors such as Ibn al-Athir and al-Dhahabi. Doubts were expressed regarding his reliability. His main concern was the Christian advance in the Iberian Peninsula, and one of his aims was to urge Eastern Muslims to go there to perform jihad, which made him quite inventive in his rendition of the Andalusi past, as I have analyzed elsewhere. Still, his information on the Almohad period was considered trustworthy by Maghribi historians such as Ibn al-Qattan and Ibn Simak.

The second case is that of 'Abd al-'Aziz ibn Shaddad ibn Mu'izz ibn Badis al-Sanhaji (d. after 600/1204), a member of the Zirid family, which ruled Ifriqiya. He participated in the Almohad conquest of al-Mahdiyya. Afterwards, he left for the East, settling in Damascus where he wrote his chronicle 'Book of compilation and explanation on the historical events of Qayrawan' (*Kitab al-jam' wa'l-bayan fi akhbar al-Qayrawan*) for Saladin. The work is lost but was quoted by later authors such as al-Tijani (d. after 1311). His portrayal of 'Abd al-Mu'min is positive, describing his piety and deep belief, of which he was a witness. In contrast, the Sevillan Ibn Samira al-Fihri (d. after 1203) concentrated on Almohad wickedness in his *Ta'rikh fi dawlat 'Abd al-Mu'min wa-hizbihi*, and perhaps for this very reason it has been lost.

Another historical work hostile to the Almohads written during 'Abd al-Mu'min's time is that of Damascene author Ibn al-Qalanisi

(d. 1160), who inserted in his history of Damascus, in the entry devoted to the year 1146, information about the Maghrib that he had obtained from some travelling Maghribi scholars and letters sent by Maghribis to their relatives. His main source was the Sicilian scholar Abu 'Abd Allah Muhammad ibn 'Abd al-Jabbar al-Siqilli. Ibn al-Qalanisi describes the Almohads as Kharijis, highlighting their bloodshed and their disregard for Islamic law. Ibn Tumart is described as versed in law and religion, known for his asceticism and abstinence from illicit things, trained in Iraq in debate and polemics. In Ibn al-Qalanisi's telling, when Ibn Tumart returned to the Maghrib, he called for the 'doctrine of discursive thinking' (*madhhab al-fikr*) and ordered the people of al-Mahdiyya to build a palace devoted to thought (*'ala niyyat al-fikra*) and to adore God in it through thought (*al-fikra*). This is a terminology we do not find in Almohad texts and it is unclear what exactly he was referring to.

The need for Arabization among the Almohad elites has already been discussed in Chapter 5, together with 'Abd al-Mu'min's efforts in this direction. It is thus not surprising to find a number of grammarians attracted to Marrakesh. Before Ibn Mada', whose activities as tutor of the caliph's sons and as judge have already been mentioned, the caliph had invited the grammarian, poet and *adib* (scholar) Ibn 'Abd al-Jalil al-Tudmiri (d. 1160), who wrote a book to facilitate the study of the Arabic language (*Kitab al-tawti'a fi l-'arabiyya*). Some of his extant verses deal with the ignorance that prevailed in the town in which he lived, in what seems to be a reference to Marrakesh. Abu l-'Abbas ibn Sayyid al-Jurawi (d. ca. 1164) was a grammarian from Málaga brought to Marrakesh by the caliph as a tutor for his children. He lived the rest of his life in the Almohad capital, having become rich and famous. Ibn Maymun al-'Abdari (d. 1172), a poet and grammarian from Córdoba, was also a tutor to 'Abd al-Mu'min's sons. He wrote a work on Ibn Tumart's *A'azz ma yutlab*, called *Sharh Kitab al-'ilm*. At one public audience held by the caliph he devoted some erotic verses to a young man from Aghmat who was present. The caliph prohibited him from attending future audiences and had him fired. The relevance given to the grammarians had to do not only with education, but also with the judicature, as a number of scholars of the Arabic language were named as judges throughout the empire, as in the case of Ibn Lubbal from Jerez (d. 1187). One of the reasons for the existence of differences of opinion in the legal sphere – which as mentioned in the previous chapter was a matter of concern for the Almohad caliphs – was an incorrect understanding of Arabic: having grammarians as judges seems to have been considered a solution to the problem.

DOCTORS, PHILOSOPHERS AND ASTRONOMERS

Among the physicians active at the Almohad court, Ibn Tufayl wrote a didactic poem on medicine that reflects the concern for education and making knowledge more widely accessible that was one of the salient characteristics of the Almohad period. This concern is also revealed in the case of Abu Marwan ibn Zuhr, known in the Latin West as Abhomerón Abinçoar (d. 1161), a member of a highly reputed family of physicians whose father had served the Almoravids. 'Abd al-Mu'min took him into his personal service and had great esteem for his knowledge on medical matters. Ibn Zuhr started writing a book on therapeutics and diet (*Kitab al-taysir fi l-mudawat wa'l-tadbir*), until one day he was visited by someone charged with supervising his activities who found his approach to the book faulty, as it would only be of use to experienced doctors. Ibn Zuhr then started writing a more accessible book focused on practical medicine, the *Kitab al-jami'*. Both his *Kitab al-taysir* and his book on dietetics (*Kitab al-aghdhiya*) were written on the suggestion of 'Abd al-Mu'min. Ibn Zuhr's writings served as a practical complement to Ibn Rushd al-Hafid's book on medical theory, the *Kulliyat fi l-tibb*, written between 1162 and 1169.

Ibn Rushd al-Hafid had joined the Almohads in his youth, later writing a work in which he explained what had led him to this decision (*Maqala fi kayfiyyat dukhulihi fi l-amr al-'aziz*). We have seen in Chapter 4 that the *talabat al-hadar* were described by al-Marrakushi as being learned in rational speculation (*'ilm al-nazar*). Ibn al-Qalanisi's description of Almohad doctrine with reference to 'thought' (*fikr*) goes in the same direction, as does Ibn Tufayl's novel, as explained at the end of the previous chapter, with its emphasis on rational thought leading to superior knowledge. Ibn Rushd al-Hafid started his studies on Aristotle during 'Abd al-Mu'min's time. Although he served 'Abd al-Mu'min's successors in different capacities (jurist, judge, physician), his main interest was in philosophy, being a supporter of the demonstrative method that opened the laws of nature up to scrutiny. The reign of the third Almohad caliph would see Ibn Rushd al-Hafid's dramatic fall from favour, commonly referred to as his 'disgrace' (*nakba*), motivated by the opposition of both the Almohad old guard – who resisted being substituted by men like him in the caliph's inner circle – and by the traditional Maliki jurists – who resisted opening the legal sphere to direct intervention by the caliph and his doctrinarians.

Under 'Abd al-Mu'min and his two successors, the caliphs supported philosophical inquiry, while claiming at the same time that they had access to a special type of knowledge as inheritors of the Mahdi. In this claim they were close to the Fatimid imam-caliphs who had also combined their special spiritual and intellectual charisma with the promotion of philosophy. In the preface to his philosophical novel, Ibn Tufayl refers to an unnamed interlocutor who asked him to explain Ibn Sina (Avicenna)'s philosophy, claiming that his questions pushed him to think in a way he had never done before, at the same time bringing about in him a state of joy and pleasure. As a member of the *talabat al-hadar*, Ibn Tufayl's mission was to answer the questions posed by the caliph or the sayyid he was serving, and he is undoubtedly referring here to 'Abd al-Mu'min's son Abu Ya'qub Yusuf, who had been trained in philosophy. 'Abd al-Mu'min himself is portrayed as a wise ruler in Ibn Tahir's work mentioned in the previous chapter. Carlos del Valle has argued that Maimonides might also have been one of the scholars in 'Abd al-Mu'min's entourage who were involved in rational speculation.

In the field of astronomy, Ahmad ibn Muhammad al-Yahsubi al-Qurtubi wrote for 'Abd al-Mu'min on the lunar mansions and their use in telling the time at night. This book, *Kitab al-tabyin fi ma'rifat dukhul al-shuhur wa'l-sinin*, belongs to the field of popular astronomy. Under 'Abd al-Mu'min's successors, Jabir ibn Aflah (sixth/twelfth century) and al-Bitruji (alive 1185–1192), a student of Ibn Tufayl, would carry out their criticism of Ptolemaic astronomy, another indication of the intellectual ferment that characterized the Almohad twelfth century. Mention has already been made of how Almohad chronicles paid attention to the architects and engineers responsible for the caliphal building projects, and in this respect it is to be noted that Ibn Tumart's *A'azz ma yutlab* pays attention to these branches of knowledge that also made possible such ingenious devices as the mobile *maqsura* in the Kutubiyya mosques and the mechanism that enabled the 'Uthmanic *mushaf* to emerge from its container. The physician Ibn Zuhr did not fall short in the field of ingenuity; 'Abd al-Mu'min hated taking purgative potions, and so Ibn Zuhr devised a way to make it easier for him. In the caliph's gardens there was a vineyard – he replaced the water used to irrigate it with water mixed with the purgative potion so that the grapes ended up containing its properties. Ibn Zuhr presented the caliph with a bunch of these grapes and made him eat ten of them; as the doctor explained, they would make the caliph defecate ten times – as indeed happened. This greatly enhanced the caliph's well-being as well as Ibn Zuhr's standing.

THE *GHURABA'*, THE MYSTICS AND THE SAINTS

In his tract equating the Almohad polity with the 'virtuous city' of the philosophers, Ibn Tahir refers to 'Abd al-Mu'min as a stranger (*gharib*). Behind this expression resonate the Prophetic traditions according to which 'Islam began as a stranger and shall return to being a stranger just as it began. Thus, blessed be the strangers!' These *hadiths* have provided solace to individuals and groups who felt spiritually alienated in the Islamic societies in which they lived: by claiming the condition of 'strangers', they made their spiritual alienation a source of strength. In the period studied here, ideals of religious and intellectual renewal had flourished, creating expectations of change that can be traced among different groups: scholars, mystics and philosophers, as I have documented elsewhere. The *gharib* could be a moderate who tried to change his immediate context verbally and through his own behaviour, or a radical who tried to effect change by seizing power. Ibn Qasi and Ibn Tumart represented this radical option, and both referred to their own group as *ghuraba'*. For the philosophers, the condition of isolation and estrangement (*ghurba*) was taken for granted as they catered to a limited number of individuals able to grasp the demonstrative method, but in the twelfth century they appear to have tried to extend their constituency.

The *ghuraba'* claimed moral superiority over the rest of society. Because they opposed the *status quo*, they were not innovators as their opponents alleged, but the true believers amidst a mass gone astray; their righteousness contrasted with the corruption and degradation of the society that surrounded them. For Ibn Qasi, universal history was divided into two cycles. The first started with Adam and ended with Jesus. Muhammad introduced the new cycle that would last one thousand years. Muslims now found themselves at the middle of that second cycle, the phase of the *ghuraba'*, those who preserved the light of Revelation after the disappearance of the Prophet. This light was not in the transmitted texts, but in the primordial source producing it: Moses had access to it when God spoke directly to him – a claim made by Ibn Qasi himself. The immediacy of contact with the Divinity that this type of mystic claimed was attractive for many in the twelfth century Islamic world: representing it, the 'friends of God' (*awliya' Allah*) considered themselves above the scholars whose knowledge came from the study of texts.

The figure of the Eastern scholar and mystic al-Ghazali, hailed as the reviver of the faith, and his polyphonic work that spoke to the believers in different ways and with different degrees of depth, are often invoked to explain such aspirations for change, but he was just one representative of them, not their only spokesman. His influence in the Islamic West and the extent to which the trends that can be detected in the twelfth century should be attributed to him have long been a matter of debate. There is no doubt that there were Andalusis and Maghribis who were influenced by his ideas, and as we have seen Ibn Tumart was presented as one of them. In my view, however, while al-Ghazali had a substantive role in the thought of scholars such as the Andalusis al-Turtushi (d. 1126) and Abu Bakr ibn al-'Arabi (d. 1148), or Ibn Hirzihim (d. 1164) in Fez, among others, his connection with the Almohad movement was established at a late stage, when the drive that had led to their victory and to the conquest of an empire had to be translated into something familiar to the scholars of the Islamic West.

In other words, al-Ghazali's role in the Almohad experience was not primordial, but rather a subsequent development that served to rally the support of those who had been attracted by his doctrines and felt disappointed when the Almoravids failed to fully embrace them. Ibn Tumlus (d. 1223), in his thought-provoking description of the intellectual dynamics of the Islamic West, stated that, after the burning of al-Ghazali's work and the persecution of his followers under the Almoravids, the Mahdi Ibn Tumart appeared, inviting his followers to study the books of al-Ghazali and making them realize that his doctrines were in agreement with his own. The process was, in my view, the opposite: Ibn Tumart's teachings, taken out of the Masmuda context in which they developed, were made intelligible to the urban conquered population by connecting them with al-Ghazali.

The Almohad experience was closer in its origins not to the Ghazalian outlook of the literate scholars from urban centres, but to the veneration of saints, those 'friends of God' that – especially in the rural areas – were illiterate or semi-literate religious figures whose role was the production not of difficult texts dealing with theological and legal matters, but of prayers and litanies that offered consolation and could be used by the believers to obtain tangible things, as well as the performance of miracles that caused amazement or solved problems. Such was the case of the Andalusi Abu Madyan (d. 1197) or the Maghribi Abu Ya'za, among many others of less renown, who similarly attracted people to them through their behaviour, as healers, soothsayers and performers of miracles (*karamat*) such as the miraculous distribution of goods, healing, control of wild beasts (especially lions), or extraordinary signs such as becoming enveloped in light. We have encountered one such figure in Chapter 4, the pious man Ibn Bughlat, whose prayer against the man in charge of the Almohad purge in Sijilmasa caused his death and set those to be executed free. Their actions were recorded in the hagiographical works that started to be written precisely in Almohad times by Maghribi authors such as al-Tamimi (d. 1206) and al-Tadili (d. 1229), and the Andalusi Tahir al-Sadafi. Al-Tadili's work is of special interest – as shown in the studies by Halima Ferhat, Fernando Rodríguez Mediano and Rachid El Hour, among others – because it covers the region where the Almohad movement started. Al-Tadili acted as judge for the Almohads, but in his work he reflected the tension between the saints and mystics and those in power, as the latter tried to profit from the former's charisma and also to keep it under control, well aware of the potential threat it posed.

We have already seen the case of Abu l-‘Abbas al-Sabti, who became a salaried Sufi under ‘Abd al-Mu'min. Ibn Rushd al-Hafid had sent someone from Córdoba to observe his behaviour and teachings. When the scout reported back, Ibn Rushd's comment was that al-Sabti's doctrine was that existence is affected by generosity, linking it to the doctrine of an unnamed ancient philosopher. Ibn Rushd does not seem to have recommended any action to take against the saint and, although the connection is not directly made by al-Tadili, it was probably after this that Abu l-‘Abbas al-Sabti received a stipend from the treasury with the *talabat al-hadar*. He wore woollen clothes and walked in the markets with a stick, beating people who failed to attend the prayers at the appropriate times – something that Ibn Tumart would have approved of.

The caliph himself is said to have sought out the help of the saint Abu Dawud Muzahim al-Badisi to cure his son's vitiligo. In a story recorded by al-Badisi (d. ca. 1322), the caliph sent a horse to bring Abu Dawud to the capital, but the saint decided to mount a donkey that travelled as fast as the horse. Once in Marrakesh, Abu Dawud put saliva on one of his fingers and asked the caliph to apply it to his son's afflicted areas, thereby curing him. The caliph then ordered money to be distributed among the poor and food to be prepared for both the common people and the elites. The caliph also offered money to the saint, who rejected it; when one of his sons accepted it instead, his father cursed him, announcing that he would die poor, as indeed happened.

‘Abd al-Mu'min's relations with saints could also be hostile, at least initially, as occurred with Abu Shu‘ayb al-Sanhaji (d. 1166) and Abu

Ya'za (d. 1177). Abu Shu'ayb al-Sanhaji was from Dukkala and taught the Qur'an. The caliph ordered that he be brought to Marrakesh after 1147, and when he saw how emaciated he was, he felt pity for him. 'Abd al-Mu'min wanted to debate with him, but having realized his special powers, placed Ibn Tumart's companion Abu Muhammad Wasnar in charge of the interrogation. When asked what *al-tawhid* was, Abu Shu'ayb answered with Qur'anic verses and cursed Wasnar, whereupon an earthquake shook 'Abd al-Mu'min's palace. The caliph realized that the saint had caused it and ordered that he be treated with respect and generosity. Abu Shu'ayb – a Sanhaja – only asked for benevolence towards the widows and children of the deposed Almoravid emir and that they be allowed to go wherever they wanted. Ibn Sahib al-salat recorded that when some relatives of his were captured by the Christians in al-Andalus, he travelled to Marrakesh to get help in having them set free. In Azemmour, he entered the mosque of Abu Shu'ayb al-Sanhaji, who was seated in prayer. Ibn Sahib al-salat started praying too, and suddenly he heard a sound like rainfall, but realized that it was the sound of the saint crying. Having told him about the plight of his relatives, Abu Shu'ayb prayed for them and before a year had passed Ibn Sahib al-salat was reunited with them in Marrakesh.

Abu Ya'za Yallanur was an illiterate Berber-speaking saint, born among the Haskura in the vicinity of the Atlas Mountains, who practiced asceticism near Tinmal for twenty years before moving to the mountains near Meknes after running into trouble with the Almohad government. Abu Ya'za was examined by 'Abd al-Mu'min, imprisoned for several days in the minaret of the Kutubiyya mosque and then freed, having accepted Almohad authority and advised his disciples to give up their resistance to it. Although ignorant of Arabic, he knew how to distinguish between those who recited the Qur'an correctly and those who did not. He readily acknowledged that he was ignorant, claiming to know only what God himself had taught him.

A scholar as closely attached to the Almohad rulers as Ibn Rushd al-Hafid was not fully attracted by al-Ghazali's doctrines nor by mysticism, although he was not necessarily hostile to them. After 'Abd al-Mu'min's time, the Almohad caliphs showed an inclination toward the Sufis, granting them an official recognition that was uncommon, as Halima Ferhat has shown, although there were also episodes of persecution. Many then left for the East, among them Muhyi l-din ibn 'Arabi (d. 1240), whose hugely influential mystical doctrines are indebted to the Almohad context in which he spent his early life.

SHIFTING TRAJECTORIES AND THE NON-ALMOHADS

The Sevillan scholar Abu Bakr ibn al-'Arabi (d. 1148) was one of those who felt that he belonged to the 'strangers' (*ghuraba'*) of his times. During his stay in the East, he had met al-Ghazali and adhered to his project of religious revival; back in Seville in 1101 and having been named judge by the Almoravid emir, he tried to introduce some changes in the legal and religious spheres, but did not succeed as he expected. As he himself explained it, he obliged people to pray and to perform the precept of commanding good and refraining from evil, and he also censured the powerful who committed illegal acts. All of them plotted together against him, even attacking and almost killing him in his own house, and eventually had him dismissed from his judgeship. Later, after the Almohads had conquered his town – in a campaign that saw one of his sons killed – he was a member of the Andalusi delegation that crossed the Strait in 1147 to pledge obedience to 'Abd al-Mu'min and also to try to negotiate the return of some of the confiscated properties.

While the delegation was in Marrakesh, news reached the caliph of an anti-Almohad rebellion in Niebla and Seville that had taken place in the meantime, and the delegates were put under surveillance. They feared for their lives but were eventually freed when the caliph was informed that the rebellion had been caused by mismanagement on the part of Ibn Tumart's brothers. The caliph even compensated the delegates with a substantial sum of money. On that occasion, Abu Bakr ibn al-'Arabi was asked by 'Abd al-Mu'min if he had ever seen the Mahdi during his stay in the East or met him in his study sessions with al-Ghazali. The Andalusi scholar answered that he had never met him, but had heard about him and that al-Ghazali had repeatedly said that there was no doubt about his appearance. Abu Bakr ibn al-'Arabi had returned from the East seven years before Ibn Tumart travelled there, so what 'Abd al-Mu'min had asked him was chronologically impossible. The Andalusi's answer was, however, very diplomatic: the figure he would have heard al-Ghazali mention was, of course, not Ibn Tumart, but the eschatological Mahdi. Abu Bakr ibn al-'Arabi died in Fez shortly after this exchange, while on his way back to al-Andalus.

We cannot know if Abu Bakr ibn al-'Arabi would have joined the Almohads, accepting *al-tawhid* like other Andalusis such as Ibn Tahir and Ibn Rushd al-Hafid or a member of the Sevillan delegation, Abu Bakr ibn al-Jadd, whose brother had been killed during the rebellion in Niebla. In Meknes, 'Abd Allah ibn Muhammad ibn Hammad ibn Zaghbush (d. 1197) also joined the Almohads: he is described as having performed emigration (*hijra*) to them – in the same way that in early Islam converts were expected to perform emigration to the Muslim camps. The Almohad conqueror of his town during the reign of 'Abd al-Mu'min had killed his father and seven of his relatives; this violence may have induced him to join the new rulers.

Abu Bakr ibn al-'Arabi's contemporary Qadi 'Iyad had preached against the Almohads when they attacked Ceuta, but when it fell, according to Qadi 'Iyad's son, he accepted *al-tawhid*, heading a delegation of notables who travelled to Salé to meet 'Abd al-Mu'min. They were lavished with hospitality and gifts, and Qadi 'Iyad was confirmed as judge of Ceuta. He later joined the rebellion against the Almohads in 1147–8, travelling to al-Andalus to pledge obedience to the Almoravid Ibn Ghaniya. When the Almohads retook Ceuta, Qadi 'Iyad was sent to Tadla as judge for the nomadic tribes and died in Marrakesh, where he eventually became one of the city's seven saints. His son Muhammad did join the Almohads and, as shown by Serrano, tried to convince his readers that his father had not given his consent to the rebellion against the Almohads, given his hatred of strife among Muslims (*fitna*).

Muhammad ibn 'Iyad, by joining the Almohads, was able to maintain his family's status as members of the religious urban elite. Former rulers who submitted, although they lost their power, could also maintain an elevated social and economic position, as happened with the ruler of Bougie who moved to Marrakesh with his family and received properties, devoting the rest of his life to hunting, lions in particular (they disappeared from the area only in the early twentieth century), which he gave as presents to the caliph. The former lord of Jerez, Abu l-Ghamr ibn 'Azzun, became a loyal ally of 'Abd al-Mu'min, and his brother, who knew both Arabic and Romance languages, was of great help in the contacts established with the Christian king of León. Mudafi' ibn Rushayd, the cultivated governor of Gabes, was treated generously and settled in Fez. Some of these lineages would later suffer because of their support for the Almohads, as happened with the Banu Wazir of the Algarve who were persecuted and killed by the anti-Almohad rebel Ibn Hud al-Mutawakkil (d. 1238).

While 'Abd al-Mu'min confided military and economic affairs mostly to the early Almohads and the Mu'minids, he soon realized that he needed to incorporate into his administration some of those who had worked for the Almoravids and also members of the conquered populations. This he did with Abu Ja'far ibn 'Atiyya and also the Andalusi Abu l-'Abbas ibn al-Saqr (d. 1173), imam of the Friday mosque in Almoravid Marrakesh, who 'Abd al-Mu'min named judge in Granada and Seville. We have seen in previous chapters how opposition to Almohad rule was repressed. Rachid Bourouiba has noted that while 'Abd al-Mu'min did not maintain any of the Almoravid or Hammadid governors in the far and central Maghrib, in Ifriqiya and al-Andalus he tended to keep those who submitted to him. The caliph's violence seems to have been especially indiscriminate in the rural areas, whereas in the more urbanized regions negotiations and alliances took place with the local elites. All this reveals the *layered sovereignty* that is characteristic of empires. The Banu Sa'id of Alcalá la Real managed to retain part of their former power once they submitted to the Almohads.

Some among the conquered did not accept Almohadism, an attitude which led to the demise of several previously influential lineages. At the same time, new urban lineages were formed, as examined by El Hour for al-Andalus. Individual opposition to Almohad doctrine on the part of scholars must in many cases have been kept private, and thus we hear of some who only prayed and taught in their own mosque. Akhyal ibn Idris al-Rundi (d. 1165), named judge of Córdoba and Seville, was exiled for some time in Meknes for having stated that the caliph had to be a Qurashi.

Those who wanted neither to convert to Almohadism nor to remain under Almohad rule had the option of leaving the empire, a topic that still merits further study. Giuseppe Mandalá, for instance, has shed light on the emigration of Jews. As regards Muslims, al-Maqqari recorded the case of Abu l-Walid Muhammad ibn 'Abd Allah ibn Khiyara (d. 1156), who in 1147 fled from Córdoba to Alexandria to escape from the Almohads, moved to the Hijaz when he thought they would also take Egypt, then travelled on to India. (This last part of the story seems to be an exaggeration, as he actually died in Yemen.) The judge and ruler of Málaga, Abu l-Hakam ibn Hassun, committed suicide in June 1152 before the Almohads took the city. His former enemy Abu 'Abd Allah ibn Simak al-'Amili – who had moved to Marrakesh after its conquest by 'Abd al-Mu'min – was named judge of Málaga by the conquerors.

There were also scholars who collaborated with the Almohads and then nevertheless left for the East, as was the case with the historian Abu Muhammad al-Ashiri (d. 1166), who left Marrakesh around the time of the caliph's death. This was also the time when Abu l-Yasa' ibn Hazm and Maimonides left for Egypt, and coincides with increasing reports of men who had left the Maghrib during 'Abd al-Mu'min's rule who now returned to the Maghrib after his death, as if the disappearance of the first Almohad caliph had reopened the flow of people between the Islamic West and East.

8

'ABD AL-MU'MIN'S SIGNIFICANCE AND LEGACY

Muhyi l-din Ibn 'Arabi, in his *Muhadarat al-abrar*, mentions the arrival of a Frankish delegation to the court of 'Abd al-Rahman III and describes the caliph wearing clothes worth only four dirhams sitting on the floor with a Qur'an, a sword and a brazier. He tells the delegation, 'God commanded us that we call you to this', pointing to the Qur'an, 'and if you refuse, we will force your submission by this', pointing to the sword, 'and if we kill you, this fire will be waiting for you', pointing to the brazier. This account does not match up with what we know about the Cordoban Umayyad caliph, but reflects instead another caliph closer to Muhyi l-din Ibn 'Arabi's times, whom his father may have met. The simplicity, the lack of pomp and the religious commitment are much more befitting of the first Almohad caliph as he has been described. The image is powerful, as is the statue of 'Abd al-Mu'min erected in his honour in Nedroma. There he appears as the conqueror he was, who possessed a strength that inspired fear and even admiration in his enemies, including the Arabs he defeated in Sétif and who transformed him into the mythical 'Khalifa al-Zanati' of the *Sirat Bani Hilal*, the saga that recorded the wanderings of the Arab Banu Hilal across the lands of North Africa.

Strong belief and fierce violence loom large in how 'Abd al-Mu'min has been represented; less so – undeservedly – his political acumen in navigating the difficult waters between Ibn Tumart's Masmuda legacy and his own dynastic ambitions, and in building an empire that

The statue of 'Abd al-Mu'min in Nedroma (courtesy of Askelaadden / Wikimedia Commons).

for the first time united the whole of North Africa and al-Andalus. 'Abd al-Mu'min should also be remembered for his foresight regarding the temporal limits of Ibn Tumart's Mahdism and the need to complement it with new sources of religious and political authority. Especially compelling is his investment in the education of his sons, and in the young generations of the early Almohads and the conquered peoples, to allow for the construction of a new world. Certainly he did not do all this alone, but part of his genius was to have found men who advised him well and to have listened to them. The new world could not stand on violence alone. Al-Idrisi had said of the Almohads that they believed that everything was permitted to them, and 'Abd al-Mu'min himself shared this opinion in the first period of his rule; the conquest of Marrakesh and of new territories progressively taught him that the rights of the vanquished had to be taken into account if he wanted the empire he was building to last.

While there were precedents for the conviction that the Maghrib was superior to other lands, it was in Almohad times when pride in being a Maghribi acquired special salience. 'Abd al-Mu'min's reign was decisive in fostering such pride, which, rooted in the establishment of a new local caliphate, involved a complex mixture of elements. For Ibn Jubayr, it resonated with the cultural achievements in Arabic of the urban scholars to whom he belonged, and with the memory of the Cordoban Umayyad caliphate. For the rural populations in al-Maghrib al-aqsa, it resonated with the elevation of one of their own to the status of Mahdi, of their local language becoming a vehicle for religious instruction and official communication, and with the foundation of a local shrine and pilgrimage. As caliph, 'Abd al-Mu'min had to address both the Arabized urban scholars, the Berber-speaking population, and eventually also the Arab tribes he had defeated, and for the most part he did so successfully. The various components with which he built the Almohad caliphate have been discussed in separate chapters in this book, but 'Abd al-Mu'min was successful because he put them together as if they came in a single package, even if they had been drawn from different sources and were targeted at different audiences. The package was singular fundamentally because it originated from the Prince of the Believers, who controlled the religious and political spheres and headed a highly centralized order that he equated with *al-amr al-'aziz*, God's order.

The main limitations to his power came from the original Almohad tribes whose shaykhs had accepted that 'Abd al-Mu'min succeed their Mahdi to avoid the danger of infighting, but who did not forget that he had been just one among others; neither did they renounce having their share in the polity they had helped to create. That share in the political, economic and religious running of the caliphate was legitimized through the figure of Ibn Tumart and his creed, in the maintenance and inviolability of which the shaykhs had a vested interest. 'Abd al-Mu'min's needs as Prince of the Believers did not clash overtly with the shaykhs' interests as he created an empire and the polity to run it. Rather, the clash occurred mainly with his descendants. The hostility between the Mu'minids and the shaykhs, who had coexisted for decades in spite of all the tensions, came to a head after 1220, greatly weakening the caliphate. By 1248, eighty-five years after 'Abd al-Mu'min's death, the great majority of al-Andalus had fallen into the hands of the Christians, with the exception of the small Nasrid kingdom of Granada. Tunis and Tlemcen became independent under the Hafsids and the Abdalwadids, respectively, and Fez fell into the hands of the Marinids, who eventually conquered Marrakesh in 1269. The Marinids and the Abdalwadids rejected Almohadism, the Hafsids did not; the Nasrids did eventually, although this story is still to be told.

In 1213, fifty years after 'Abd al-Mu'min's death and twelve years before the birth of Thomas Aquinas (1225–1274), Ibn Tumart's creed was translated into Latin by Marcos of Toledo at the request of Rodrigo Jiménez de Rada, archbishop of Toledo. 'Abd al-Mu'min had not managed to make every one of his subjects learn it by heart, but the empire he built made Christendom aware that something new was afoot among the Muslims, and that it was somehow related to what they believed and why. Rodrigo Jiménez de Rada remarked that Ibn Tumart had managed to prove the Unicity of God, the first and prime mover of everything, by simply relying on necessary assertions, while the texts in the Qur'an were incoherent and confusing. This was the beginning of an interest in Almohad thought that reached its peak in the reception of Ibn Rushd al-Hafid's (Averroes's) commentaries on Aristotle in Latin Christendom and in Thomas Aquinas's Averroism. The political and intellectual project of the king of Castille, Alfonso X (r. 1252–1284), can be better understood by taking into account the preceding Almohad polity, as I have explained elsewhere.

Before that, the Almohad creed, with its emphasis on reason and the intriguing nature of Ibn Tumart's and 'Abd al-Mu'min's trajectories, constituted the background against which Ibn Tufayl had produced a philosophical novel on how man by the sheer power of his intellect can reach an understanding of God, adding that if coupled with a mystical experience he could elevate himself beyond human limits. Written towards the end of 'Abd al-Mu'min's caliphate, Ibn Tufayl's tale, ripe for a multitude of possible readings, would have a lasting impact on the European Enlightenment, while at the same time signalling various pathways for the future of Almohadism.

One of these was to pay attention to Aristotelian philosophy, already developed in al-Andalus under Ibn Bajja in Almoravid times. Ibn Tumart's conception of God could be understood in such a way as to give religious justification to the study of philosophy and lead to the development of a positive view of the laws of nature as the expression of God's governance of the world. This was the path followed by Ibn Rushd al-Hafid (Averroes), who as a young man had joined the Almohads during 'Abd al-Mu'min's caliphate. In his effort to counterbalance the Almohad shaykhs, the Prince of the Believers fostered the formation of a corps of doctrinarians, the *talaba*, who were dependent on him. Those directly attached to him, the *talabat al-hadar*, included in their activities philosophical discussions that were kept within close circles according to Ibn Tufayl's recommendations. 'Abd al-Mu'min seems to have been aware that his descendants would need philosophy to claim for themselves the capacity to ensure knowledge of the Truth in a way that made them independent from the shaykhs, with their exclusive reliance on Ibn Tumart. During the reign of the second caliph, Ibn Rushd al-Hafid's work as a commentator of Aristotle was to have a lasting impact not only on Latin Christendom but also on Judaism, mainly through the work of Maimonides, who like Ibn Rushd had joined the Almohad movement in his youth. The impact was more limited in the Islamic world, especially after Ibn Rushd al-Hafid suffered persecution triggered by the Almohad shaykhs, who resented the third Almohad caliph publicly giving the philosopher priority over them.

Another path was philosophical mysticism, with its longstanding tradition in al-Andalus that would culminate with Muhyi l-din Ibn 'Arabi. But while philosophy could be more easily controlled, as it was by necessity confined to small circles of thinkers, mystics were attractive to the masses, who sometimes granted them not only religious but also political authority in a way that opened the possibility for new Mahdis to arise. Both philosophy and Mahdism opened the door to think about prophecy. While Aristotelian philosophy could lead one to doubt the veracity of prophecy, Mahdism could lead one to doubt, if not its veracity, then at least its finality. This second type of doubt could, however, be more easily channelled in a way that did not endanger the figure of the Prophet Muhammad, on which the truth of Islam was founded. While mystics were persecuted under the Almohads as under previous polities, some of them could also be co-opted and even receive an official salary, especially when they were willing to protect prophecy, for example by attaching themselves to the Prophetic lineage or by formulating their doctrines without overtly claiming superiority over the Prophet. Almohadism brings to the fore the acknowledgment that prophecy, with its seminal place in Islam, has often proved to be a contested arena.

When dealing with Ibn Tumart's thought, most scholars end up employing the word 'syncretic' to describe it. As I have explained, although it is difficult to reconstruct exactly what Ibn Tumart's thought consisted of, it is much easier to analyze how it was used and transformed by the man who ensured Ibn Tumart's legacy. That man, of course, was 'Abd al-Mu'min. Roger Le Tourneau and Ambrosio Huici Miranda considered him responsible for the eventual failure of the Almohad caliphate through his decision to incorporate the Arabs into the Almohad army, thus shaking off the Berber character of the early movement, and Henri Terrasse pointed to the inevitable failure of an empire spanning such disparate societies as those of al-Andalus and the Maghrib. While these interpretations remain open to discussion, what is undeniable is that without 'Abd al-Mu'min, the careers of Ibn Tufayl, Ibn Rushd al-Hafid, Muhyi l-din Ibn 'Arabi, Maimonides and many other scholars and thinkers would never have been possible.

SOURCES AND SELECT BIBLIOGRAPHY

The full bibliography for this work can be found at oneworld-publications.com/abd-al-mu-min-hb.html.

SOURCES

ʿAbd al-Muʾmin, *Rasāʾil*, in *Un recueil de lettres officielles almohades* (Paris: 1942); also in *Rasāʾil muwaḥḥidiyya: Majmūʿa jadīda*, ed. A. al-ʿAzzāwī (Kenitra: 2 vols., 1995–2001).

ʿAbd al-Wāḥid al-Marrākushī (d. after 1224), *al-Muʿjib fī talkhīṣ akhbār al-Maghrib*, ed. R. Dozy (Amsterdam: 1968); Spanish trans. A. Huici Miranda (Tetouan: 1955).

Anonymous (13th century), *Kitāb al-ansāb*, in *Documents inédits d'histoire almohade (Fragments manuscrits du "legajo" 1919 arabe de l'Escurial)*, ed. E. Lévi-Provençal (Paris: 1928).

al-Bādisī (d. *ca.* 1322), *al-Maqṣad al-sharīf wa'l-manzaʿ al-laṭīf fī dhikr ṣulaḥāʾ al-Rīf*, ed. Saʿīd Aʿrāb (Rabat: 1988); French trans. G. S. Colin, *Vies des saints du Rif* (Paris: 1926).

al-Baydhaq (12th century), 'Memoirs', in *Documents inédits d'histoire almohade (Fragments manuscrits du "legajo" 1919 arabe de l'Escurial)*, ed. E. Lévi-Provençal (Paris: 1928).

Chronica Adephonsi Imperatoris, ed. L. Sánchez Belda (Madrid: 1950).

al-Dhahabī (d. 1348), *Taʾrīkh al-Islām*, ed. Bashshār ʿAwwād Maʿrūf (Beirut: 18 vols., 2003–4).

Ibn Abī Zarʿ (d. between 1310 and 1320), *Rawḍ al-qirṭās*, ed. ʿAbd al-Wahhāb ibn Manṣūr (Rabat: 1992); Spanish trans. A. Huici Miranda (Valencia: 1964).

Ibn al-Athīr (d. 1233), *Kitāb al-Kāmil fī l-ta'rīkh*, ed. C. J. Tornberg (Leiden: 14 vols., 1851–76).

Ibn al-Ghāzī (d. 1513), *al-Rawḍ al-hatūn fī akhbār Miknāsat al-zaytūn*, ed. A. Benmansour, 2nd edition (Rabat: 1988).

Ibn 'Idhārī (d. *ca.* 1320), *al-Bayān al-mughrib fī akhbār al-Andalus wa'l-Maghrib. Qism al-muwahhidīn*, ed. M. I. al-Kattānī et al. (Beirut/Casablanca: 1985); Spanish trans. A. Huici Miranda (Tetouan: 1953–4).

Ibn Jubayr (d. 1217), *Riḥla*, ed. W. Wright; 2nd ed. revised by M. J. de Goeje (Leiden/London: 1907; repr. New York: 1973); English trans. R. J. C. Broadhurst (London: 1952).

Ibn Khaldūn (d. 1406), *Muqaddima*, trans. F. Rosenthal, 2nd ed. (London: 3 vols., 1967).

Ibn Marzūq (d. 1379), *Al-Musnad al-ṣaḥīḥ al-ḥasan*, ed. M. J. Viguera (Algiers: 1981); Spanish trans. M. J. Viguera (Madrid: 1977).

Ibn al-Qalānisī (d. 1160), *Dhayl Ta'rīkh Dimashq*, ed. H. F. Amedroz (Leiden: 1908).

Ibn al-Qaṭṭān (d. after 1252), *Naẓm al-jumān fī akhbār al-zamān*, ed. M. A. Makkī, 2nd ed. (Beirut: 1990).

Ibn al-Qifṭī (d. 1248), *Ta'rīkh al-ḥukamā'*, ed. A. Müller and J. Lippert (Leipzig: 1903).

Ibn Ṣāḥib al-ṣalāt (d. after 1197), *al-Mann bi'l-imāma*, ed. 'Abd al-Hādī al-Tāzī (Beirut: 1964); Spanish trans. A. Huici Miranda (Valencia: 1969).

Ibn Sa'īd al-Maghribī (d. 685/1286), *al-Mughrib fī ḥulā l-Maghrib*, ed. Shawqī Ḍayf (Cairo: 2 vols., 1953–5).

Ibn Simāk (8th/14th–9th/15th centuries), *al-Ḥulal al-mawshiyya*, ed. 'Abd al-Qādir Būbāya (Beirut: 2010); Spanish trans. A. Huici Miranda (Tetouan: 1951).

Ibn Tūmart (d. 1130), *A'azz mā yutlab*, ed. D. Luciani (Algiers: 1903); ed. 'Ammār Ṭālibī (Algiers: 1985); ed. 'Abd al-Ghanī Abū l-'Azm (Marrakech: 1997).

Ibn Ṭumlūs (d. 1222), *Kitāb al-madkhal li-ṣinā'at al-manṭiq*, ed. and Spanish trans. M. Asín Palacios (Madrid: 1916); ed. and French trans. M. Aouad (Paris: 2006).

al-Idrīsī (d. *ca.* 1164), *Nuzhat al-mushtāq fī khtirāq al-āfāq*, ed. and trans. R. Dozy and M. J. Goeje, *Description de l'Afrique et de l'Espagne par Edrīsī* (Leiden: 1866; repr. Amsterdam: 1969).

al-Maqqarī (d. 1632), *Nafḥ al-ṭīb min ghuṣn al-Andalus al-raṭīb*, ed. I. 'Abbās (Beirut: 8 vols., 1968).

al-Marrākushī, 'Abd al-Wāḥid (d. after 1224), *Kitāb al-mu'jib fī talkhīṣ akhbār al-Maghrib*, ed. R. Dozy (Leiden: 1881; repr. Amsterdam: 1968); ed. M. Sa'īd al-'Aryān and M. al-'Arabī al-'Alamī (Casablanca: 1978).

The Koran Interpreted, trans. A. J. Arberry (London: 1964).

al-Tamīmī (d. 1206), *al-Mustafād min manāqib al-'ubbād bi-madīnat Fās wa-mā yalīhā min al-bilād*, ed. M. al-Sharīf (Tetouan: 2 vols., 2002).
al-Tijānī (d. after 1311), *Riḥla*, ed. Ḥ. Ḥ. 'Abd al-Wahhāb (Tunis: 1981).
al-Yūsī (d. 1691), *Muḥāḍarāt*, ed. M. Ḥajjī and A. Sharqāwī (Beirut: 2 vols., 1982); English trans. J. Stearns (New York: 2020).

SELECT BIBLIOGRAPHY

Acién Almansa, Manuel, 'Cerámica y propaganda en época almohade', *Arqueología Medieval* 4 (1996), pp. 183–191.
Aguilar Sebastián, Victoria, 'La política de 'Abd al-Mu'min con los árabes de Ifrīqiya', *Actas del II Coloquio Hispano-Marroquí de Ciencias Históricas* (Madrid: 1992), pp. 17–30.
Aguilar Sebastián, Victoria, 'Estudio de historiografía almohade. Un cronista al inicio de una dinastía: al-Bayḏaq', in C. Vázquez de Benito and M. A. Manzano Rodríguez (eds.), *Actas de XVI congreso UEAI* (Salamanca: 1995), pp. 11–21.
A'rāb, Sa'īd, 'Mawqif al-muwaḥḥidīn min kutub al-furū' wa-ḥaml al-nās 'alà l-maḏhab al-ḥazmī', *Da'wat al-ḥaqq* 249 (1985), pp. 26–30.
Ayala Martínez, Carlos de, *Ibn Tūmart, el arzobispo Jiménez de Rada y la 'Cuestión sobre Dios'* (Madrid: 2017).
Baadj, Amar S., 'Evidence for the Ayyūbid *Iqṭā'* in Ifrīqiyya and a Reconsideration of the Almohad *Iqṭā'*', *Al-Masāq* 32 (2019), pp. 1–16.
Basset, Henri and Terrasse, Henri, *Sanctuaires et fortresses almohades* (Paris: 2001).
Benelhaj Soulami, Jaafar, 'La chancellerie almohade de Tinmāl: l'imām Ibn Tūmart et la formation de la structure de la lettre almohade (515/1121–524/1129)', *Arabica* 66 (2019), pp. 327–340.
Benhima, Yassir, 'Du *tamyîz* a l'*i'tirâf*: usages et légitimation du massacre au début de l'époque almohade', *Annales Islamologiques* 43 (2009), pp. 137–153.
Benhima, Yassir, 'Notes sur l'évolution de l'*iqtâ'* au Maghreb médiéval', *Al-Andalus-Magreb* 16 (2009), pp. 27–44.
Bennison, Amira K., 'The Almohads and the Qur'ān of 'Uthmān: The Legacy of the Umayyads of Cordoba in the Twelfth Century Maghrib', *Al-Masâq* 19/2 (2007), pp. 131–154.
Bennison, Amira K., 'Tribal identities and the formation of the Almohad élite: the salutory tale of Ibn 'Aṭiyya', in *EOBA. XVII*, ed. M. Méouak, *Biografías magrebíes* (Madrid: 2012), pp. 245–271.

Biblioteca de al-Andalus, ed. J. Lirola and J. M. Puerta Vílchez, 7 vols. & vol. A and B (Almería: 2004–13).

Bombrun, Loïc, ‘Les *Mémoires d’al-Bayḏaq*: l’écriture de l’histoire à l’époque almohade’, in A. Nef and M É. Voguet (eds.), *La légitimation du pouvoir au Maghreb médiéval* (Madrid: 2011), pp. 93–108.

Bongianino, Umberto, *The origin and development of Maghribī round scripts. Arabic palaeography in the Islamic West (4th/10th–6th/12th centuries)*, 2 vols., Ph.D. Thesis, Oxford, 2017.

Bourouiba, Rachid, *'Abd al-Mu'min, flambeau des Almohades* (Algiers: 1974).

Brett, Michael, ‘The Lamp of the Almohads: Illumination as a Political Idea in Twelfth-century Morocco’, in M. Brett, *Ibn Khaldun and the Medieval Maghrib* (Aldershot: 1999), pp. 1–27.

Buresi, Pascal, ‘Les cultes rendus à la tombe du mahdī Ibn Tūmart à Tinmāl (XIIe–XIIIe s.)’, *Comptes rendus des séances de l’Académie des Inscriptions et Belles-Lettres* 152/1 (2008), pp. 391–438.

Buresi, Pascal, ‘D’une Péninsule á l’autre: Cordoue, 'Uṯmān (644–656) et les arabes á l’époque almohade (XIIe–XIIIe siecle)’, *Al-Qanṭara* 31 (2010), pp. 7–29.

Calvo Capilla, Susana, ‘Peregrination and ceremonial in the Almohad mosque of Tinmal’, in L. Korn (ed.), *Encompassing the sacred* (Wiesbaden: 2020), pp. 81–106.

Cressier, Patrice, Maribel Fierro and Luis Molina (eds.), *Los Almohades: Problemas y perspectivas*, 2 vols. (Madrid: 2005).

Cressier, Patrice and Vicente Salvatierra (eds.), *Las Navas de Tolosa, 1212–2012. Miradas cruzadas* (Jaén: 2012).

Déléry, Claire, *Dynamiques économiques sociales et culturelles d’al-Andalus à partir d’une étude de la céramique de cuerda seca (seconde moitié du Xe siècle – première moitié du XIIIe siècle)*, PhD Thesis, Université de Toulouse II, 2006.

Dessus Lamare, Alfred, ‘Le *muṣḥaf* de la mosquée de Cordoue et son mobilier mecanique’, *Journal asiatique* 230 (1938), pp. 551–575.

Deverdun, Gaston, *Marrakech des origines à 1912*, 2 vols. (Rabat: 1959–66).

Ebstein, Michael, ‘Was Ibn Qasi a Sufi?’, *Studia Islamica* 11 (2015), pp. 196–232.

El Hour, Rachid, ‘Quelques reflexions sur la trajectoire intellectuelle des saints d’après *al-Tachawwuf ilā rijāl al-taṣawwuf* d’al-Tādilī’, *Mélanges Halima Ferhat* (Rabat: 2005), pp. 23–43.

Encyclopaedia of Islam Three.

Encyclopédie Berbère.

Estudios Onomástico-Biográficos de al-Andalus (EOBA). IX, ed. M. Fierro and M. L. Ávila, *Biografías almohades I* (Madrid: 1999); *EOBA. X*, ed. M. L. Ávila and M. Fierro, *Biografías almohades II* (Madrid/Granada: 2000).

Ettahiri, Ahmed S., Abdallah Fili and Jean-Pierre van Staëvel, 'Igîlîz, le *ribât* des Hargha: aux origines de l'architecture défensive des Almohades', *Hespéris-Tamuda*, LII (2017), pp. 81–107.

Ewert, Christian and J.-P. Wisshak, *Forschungen zur almohadischen Moschee. II. Die Moschee von Tinmal*, 2 vols. (Mayence: 1984).

Ferhat, Halima, *Le Maghreb aux XIIe et XIIIe siècles: Les siècles de la foi* (Rabat: 1993).

Fierro, Maribel, 'La falsificación de la historia: al-Yasaʿ b. Ḥazm y su *Kitāb al-mugrib*', *Al-Qanṭara* XVI (1995), pp. 15–38.

Fierro, Maribel, *The Almohad revolution. Politics and religion in the Islamic West during the twelfth-thirteenth centuries* (Ashgate: 2012).

Fierro, Maribel, 'Again on forced conversion in the Almohad period', in M. García-Arenal and J. Glazer-Eytan (eds.), *Forced Conversion in Christianity, Judaism and Islam* (Leiden: 2019), pp. 111–132.

Fierro, Maribel, 'Ibn Ṭufayl's *Ḥayy ibn Yaqẓān*: an Almohad Reading', *Islam and Christian-Muslim Relations* 31/4 (2020), pp. 385–405.

Fletcher, Madeleine de Gogorza, 'The anthropological context of Almohad history', *Hespéris-Tamuda* XXVI–XXVII (1988–9), pp. 25–51.

Fletcher, Madeleine, 'The Almohad *Tawḥīd*: Theology which relies on Logic', *Numen* 38/1 (1991), pp. 110–127.

Fletcher, Madeleine, 'Ibn Tūmart's teachers: the relationship with al-Ghazālī', *Al-Qanṭara* XVIII (1997), pp. 305–330.

Fili, Abdallah and Jean-Pierre van Staëvel, 'Avant Tinmal: notes historiques et archéologiques à propos d'Îgîlîz-des-Hargha, berceau du mouvement almohade', in *30 ans d'archéologie marocaine. Actes des Journées d'hommage à Madame Joudia Benslimane, (INSAP, Rabat, 8 et 9 décembre 2005)* (Rabat: 2016), pp. 326–352.

Fontenla, Salvador, 'Numismática y propaganda almohades', *Al-Qanṭara* XVIII (1997), pp. 447–462.

Fricaud, Émile, 'Les *ṭalaba* dans la société almohade (le temps d'Averroès)', *Al-Qanṭara* XVIII (1997), pp. 331–388.

Fricaud, Émile, 'Origine de l'utilisation privilégiée du terme *amr* chez les Mu'minides almohades', *Al-Qanṭara* XXIII (2002), pp. 93–122.

Fromherz, Allen J., *The Almohads: The Rise of an Islamic Empire* (London/New York: 2010).

García, Senén, 'The Masmuda Berbers and Ibn Tumart: An Ethnographic Interpretation of the Rise of the Almohad Movement', *Ufahamu: A Journal of African Studies* 18/1 (1990), pp. 3–23.

Garulo, Teresa, 'La poesía de al-Andalus en época almohade', in *Música y poesía. El Legado andalusí* (Barcelona: 1995), pp. 149–160.

Gellner, Ernst, *Muslim Society* (Cambridge: 1983).

Ghouirgate, Mehdi, *L'ordre almohade (1120–1269): une nouvelle lecture anthropologique* (Toulouse: 2014).

Ghouirgate, Mehdi, 'Le berbère au Moyen Âge. Une culture linguistique en voie de reconstitution', *Annales Histoire, Sciences Sociales* 70e année, 3 (2015), pp. 577–605.

Ghouirgate, Mehdi, '*Asmās*: le plat emblématique des Almohades', *Arabica* 62 (2015), pp. 1–22.

Ghouirgate, Mehdi, 'Réflexions autour du nom Ibn Tūmart', in Villalba Sola, D. (ed.), *Al-Muwahhidūn*, pp. 60–75 (French), pp. 279–291 (Spanish).

Hamès, Constant, 'Le pouvoir dynastique almohade entre parenté berbère, arabe et islamique', in Cressier, P. et al. (eds.), *Los Almohades*, pp. 426–450.

Hendrickson, Jocelyn, 'Prohibiting the Pilgrimage: Politics and Fiction in Mālikī Fatwās', *Islamic Law and Society* 23 (2016), pp. 161–238.

Hopkins, J. F. P., *Medieval Muslim Government in Barbary until the Sixth Century of the Hijra* (London: 1958).

Huici Miranda, Ambrosio, *Historia política del imperio almohade*, 2 vols., Tetuán, 1956–7. Repr. with introduction by E. Molina López and V. N. Oltra, 2 vols., (Granada: 2000).

Jones, Linda, 'The Christian companion: a rhetorical trope in the narration of intra-Muslim conflict during the Almohad epoch', *Anuario de Estudios Medievales* 38 (2008), pp. 793–829.

Jones, Linda, 'The Preaching of the Almohads: Loyalty and Resistance across the Strait of Gibraltar', *Medieval Encounters* 19 (2013), pp. 71–101.

Khiyara, Youssef, 'La mosquée dynastique de Tinmel: Note pour une réévaluation chronologique', in *30 ans d'archéologie marocaine. Actes des Journées d'hommage à Madame Joudia Benslimane, (INSAP, Rabat, 8 et 9 décembre 2005)* (Rabat: 2016), pp. 411–414.

Kisaichi, M., 'The Almohad social-political system or hierarchy in the reign of Ibn Tumart', *Memoirs of the Research Department of the Toyo Bunko* 48 (1990), pp. 81–101.

Le Tourneau, Roger, 'Du mouvement almohade à la dynastie mu'minide: la révolte des frères d'Ibn Tumart de 1153 à 1156', in *Hommage à G. Marçais* (Paris: 1956), II, pp. 111–116.

Le Tourneau, Roger, 'Un personnage important du mouvement almohade: Abû Hafs 'Umar Inti', *Atti del I Congresso Internazionale di Studi Nord-Africani* (Cagliari, 22–25 janv. 1965) (Cagliari: 1965), pp. 195–204.

Lévi-Provençal, Évariste, 'Ibn Tūmart et 'Abd al-Mumin. Le "fakīh du Sūs" et le "flambeau des Almohades"', *Memorial Henri Basset, II* (Paris: 1928), pp. 21–37.

Lintz, Yannick, Claire Déléry and Bulle Tuil Leonetti (eds.), *Le Maroc médiéval. Un empire de l'Afrique à l'Espagne* (Paris: 2014).

Madelung, Wilfred, 'Some notes on non-Isma'ili shiism in the Maghrib', *Studia Islamica* XLIV (1976), pp. 87–97.

Marín, Manuela, 'En los márgenes de la ley: el consumo de alcohol en al-Ándalus', in *EOBA. XIII*, ed. C. de la Puente, *Identidades marginales* (Madrid: 2003).

Marín, Manuela, 'El califa almohade: una presencia activa y benéfica', in P. Cressier et al. (eds.), *Los Almohades*, pp. 451–476.

Marinho, J. Rodrigues, 'The beginning of the characteristic Almohad coinage: some hypotheses', in I. A. Carradice (ed.), *Proceedings of the 10th International Congress of Numismatics* (London: 1986), pp. 430–436.

Martínez-Núñez, María Antonia, 'Epigrafía y propaganda almohades', *Al-Qanṭara* XVIII (1997), pp. 415–446.

Massé, Henri, 'La profession de foi et les guides spirituels de Mahdi Ibn Toumert', in *Mémorial Henri Basset*, 2 vols., (Paris: 1928), vol. 2, pp. 105–121.

Meunié, Jacques and Henri Terrasse, *Recherches Archéologiques a Marrakech* (Paris: 1952).

Mitha, Farouk, *Al-Ghazali and the Ismailis. A debate on reason and authority in Medieval Islam* (London/New York: 2001).

Molina, Luis, 'Instituciones administrativas: visires y secretarios', in M. J. Viguera (ed.), *El retroceso territorial de al-Andalus*, pp. 149–167.

Mūsā, 'Izz al-dīn Aḥmad, *Al-nashāt al-iqtiṣādī fī l-maghrib al-islāmī khilāl al-qarn al-sādis al-hijrī* (Beirut: 2003; 1st ed., 1983).

Nagel, Tilman, 'Le Mahdisme d'Ibn Tumart et d'Ibn Qasi: une analyse phénoménologique', *Revue des mondes musulmans et de la Méditerranée* 91(94) (2000), pp. 125–136.

Navarro Palazón, Julio and Jiménez Castillo, Pedro, *Siyasa. Estudio arqueológico del despoblado andalusí (ss. XI–XIII)* (Granada: 2007).

Navarro Palazón, Julio, Garrido Carretero, Fidel, Torres Carbonell, José Manuel, and Triki, Hamid, 'Agua, arquitectura y poder en una capital del Islam: la finca real del Agdal de Marrakech (ss. XII–XX)', *Arqueología de la arquitectura* 10 (2013).

Ngom, Fallou, *Muslims beyond the Arab World: The Odyssey of 'Ajami and the Muridiyya* (New York: 2016).

Peña, Salvador, 'El término de origen coránico *amr Allāh* ("Disposición de Dios") y el linguocentrismo trascendente islámico, en torno al siglo XII', *Anaquel de Estudios Arabes* 22 (2011), pp. 197–224.

Rius, Mònica, *La alquibla en al-Andalus y al-Magrib al-aqṣà* (Barcelona: 2000).

Rodríguez Mañas, Francisco, 'Charity and Deceit: The Practice of *iṭ'ām al-ṭa'ām* in Moroccan Sufism', *Studia Islamica* 91 (2000), pp. 59–90.

Rodríguez Mediano, Fernando, 'Biografías almohades en el *Tašawwuf* de al-Tādilī', in *EOBA. X*, pp. 167–193.

Ruas, M.-P., J. Ros, J.-F. Terral, S. Ivorra, H. Andrianarinosy, A. S. Ettahiri, A. Fili and J. P. van Staëvel, ‘History and Archaeology of the emblematic Argan tree in the medieval Anti-Atlas Mountains (Morocco)’, *Quaternary International* XXX (2015), pp. 1–23.

Salinger, Gerard, ‘A Christian Muḥammad legend and a Muslim Ibn Tūmart legend in the 13th century’, *Zeitschrift der Deutschen Morgenländischen Gesellschaft* 117 (1967), pp. 318–328.

Samsó, Julio, *Las ciencias de los antiguos en al-Andalus*, 2nd ed. (Almería: 2011).

Sedra, Moulay Driss, ‘La fondation du Ribat de Taza’, *Al-Andalus-Magreb* 14 (2007), pp. 203–223.

Sedra, Moulay Driss, ‘La ville de Rabat au Vie/Xiie siècle: le projet d’une nouvelle capitale de l’Empire almohade?’, *Al-AndalusMagreb* 15 (2008), pp. 275–303.

Serrano, Delfina, ‘Los Banu ʿIyad, de la caída del imperio almorávid a la instauración de la dinastía nazarí’, in *EOBA. X*, pp. 351–406.

Serrano, Delfina, ‘¿Por qué llamaron antropomorfistas a los almorávides?’, in P. Cressier et al. (eds.), *Los Almohades*, pp. 815–852.

Terrasse, Henri, *L’art hispano-mauresque des origines aux XIIIe siècle* (Paris: 1932).

Thiele, Jan, ‘Facing the Mahdī’s True Belief: Abū ʿAmr al-Salālijī’s Ashʿarite Creed and the Almohads’ Claim to Religious Authority’, *Al-ʿUṣūr al-Wusṭā* 26 (2018), pp. 96–112.

Urvoy, Dominique, ‘La pensée d’Ibn Tūmart’, *Bulletin d’Études Orientales* XXVII (1974), pp. 19–44.

Urvoy, Dominique, ‘Effets pervers du *ḥajj*, d’après le cas d’al-Andalus’, in I. R. Netton (ed.), *Golden Roads. Migration, Pilgrimage and Travel in Mediaeval and Modern Islam* (Wiltshire: 1993), pp. 43–53.

Valle, Carlos del, ‘The Jews of al-Andalus under Almohad rule’, *Iberia Judaica* 1 (2009), pp. 49–54.

van Staëvel, Jean-Pierre, ‘La caverne, refuge de ‘l’ami de Dieu’: une forme particulière de l’érémitisme au temps des Almoravides et des Almohades (Maghreb extrême, Xie–XIIIe siècles)’, *Cuadernos de Madinat al-Zahra’* 7 (2010), pp. 311–325.

van Staëvel, Jean-Pierre, ‘La foi peut-elle soulever les montagnes?’, *Revue des Mondes Musulmans et de la Méditerranée* 135 (2014), pp. 49–76.

van Staëvel, Jean-Pierre, ‘L’art almohade fut-il révolutionnaire?’, *Perspective. Actualité en histoire de l’art* 2 (2017), pp. 81–102.

van Staëvel, Jean-Pierre and Fili, Abdallah, ‘*Wa-waṣalnā ʿalā barakat Allāh ilā Īgīlīz*: à propos de la localisation d’Īgīlīz-Des-Harga, le *ḥiṣn* du Mahdī Ibn Tūmart’, *Al-Qanṭara* XXVII (2006), pp. 153–194.

van Staëvel, Jean-Pierre and Abdallah Fili, 'Centres de pouvoir dans le Sous (Maroc) au Moyen Âge: un premier inventaire d'après les textes et l'archéologie', in C. Briand-Ponsart (ed.), *Centres de pouvoir et organisation de l'espace.* Actes du *Xe colloque international sur l'histoire et l'archéologie de l'Afrique du Nord antique et médiévale* (Caen: 2014), pp. 117–140.

Vega Martín, Miguel, Salvador Peña Martín and Manuel C. Feria García, *El mensaje de las monedas almohades: numismática, traducción y pensamiento* (Cuenca: 2002).

Verskin, Alain, 'Medieval Jewish perspectives on Almohad persecutions: memory, repression and impact', in M. García-Arenal and J. Glazer-Eytan (eds.), *Forced Conversion in Christianity, Judaism and Islam. Coercion and faith in premodern Iberia and beyond* (Leiden/Boston: 2019), pp. 155–173.

Viguera, María Jesús (ed.), *El retroceso territorial de al-Andalus. Almorávides y almohades. Historia de España Menéndez Pidal*, t. VIII/2, (Madrid: 1997).

Viguera Molíns, María Jesús, 'Narrar la violencia: pasajes de la crónica de Ibn Ṣâḥib al-ṣalât sobre los almohades', in *EOBA. XIV*, ed. M. Fierro, *De muerte violenta. Política, religión y violencia en al-Andalus* (Madrid: 2004).

Villalba Sola, Dolores, *La Senda de Los Almohades. Arquitectura y Patrimonio* (Granada: 2015).

Villalba Sola, Dolores (ed.), *Al-Muwahhidūn. El despertar del califato almohade* (Granada: 2019).

Vimercati Sanseverino, Ruggero, 'La naissance de l'hagiographie marocaine: le milieu soufi de Fès et le *Mustafād* d'al-Tamīmī (m. 603/1206)', *Arabica* 61 (2014), pp. 287–308.

Zadeh, Travis, 'From Drops of Blood: Charisma and Political Legitimacy in the *translation of* the 'Uthmānic codex of al-Andalus', *Journal of Arabic Literature* 39/3 (2008), pp. 321–346.

INDEX